CURIOUS LISTS for Kids

ANIMALS

For all the animals: Wellington, Monty,
Meg, Anna, and King Boingy III.

A Raspberry Book
Editorial: Kath Jewitt
Cover design and art direction:
Sidonie Beresford-Browne
Internal design: Peter Clayman

KINGFISHER
LONDON & NEW YORK

Text and design copyright © Raspberry Books Ltd 2020
First published 2020 in the United States by Kingfisher,
120 Broadway, New York, NY 10271
Kingfisher is an imprint of
Macmillan Children's Books, London
All rights reserved.

Distributed in the U.S. and Canada by Macmillan,
120 Broadway, New York, NY 10271

Library of Congress Cataloging-in-Publication Data has been applied for.

ISBN 978-0-7534-7624-6

Kingfisher books are available for special promotions and premiums.
For details contact: Special Markets Department, Macmillan, 120 Broadway,
New York, NY 10271

For more information, please visit
www.kingfisherbooks.com

Printed in China
1 3 5 7 9 8 6 4 2
1TR/0720/WKT/RV/128MA

CURIOUS LISTS for Kids ANIMALS

Tracey Turner ✳ Caroline Selmes

KINGFISHER
LONDON & NEW YORK

5 KINGDOMS OF LIVING THINGS

Everything that's alive in the world can be divided into these five kingdoms:

1. **MONERA**—single-celled organisms such as bacteria.

2. **PROTISTS**—single-celled organisms that contain a nucleus and moving parts. Algae and molds are protists.

3. **FUNGI**—multi-celled living things that get their energy from food, like animals do. Mushrooms and yeasts are fungi.

4. **PLANTS**—multi-celled living things that make their energy from sunlight.

5. **ANIMALS**—multi-celled living things that feed on other organisms to live. There's an astonishing variety, and they're what this book is all about.

7 BIG CATS

There are 38 different types of cat in the world, and most are quite small. Not these big furry beauties, though. The Siberian tiger is the biggest of all, and weighs as much as five average people.

1. **Siberian tiger**—up to 794 pounds (360 kg)

2. **African lion**—up to 440 pounds (200 kg)

3. **Jaguar**—up to 220 pounds (100 kg)

4. **Cougar or mountain lion**—up to 187 pounds (85 kg)

5. **Leopard**—up to 176 pounds (80 kg)

6. **Snow leopard**—up to 121 pounds (55 kg)

7. **Cheetah**—up to 100 pounds (45 kg)

④ Animal HEROES

1. A pigeon named Cher Ami (French for Dear Friend) was awarded a French medal for heroism during World War I because it delivered a message that saved the lives of 194 soldiers, despite being wounded by gunfire as the enemy tried to shoot it down.

2. There have been many reports of dolphins saving people from drowning or shark attack. One happened in 2004, when a man, his daughter, and two other children were swimming off the coast of New Zealand and found themselves surrounded by dolphins. They soon realized that the dolphins were protecting them from a circling great white shark, which eventually swam away.

3. The Dickin medal has been awarded to animals in wartime 67 times, including to Beauty, a fox terrier who rescued people from bombed buildings in London during World War II.

4. Trakr the Canadian police dog was brought out of retirement to help recovery work in New York after the 2001 World Trade Center attacks. Trakr searched for survivors for two days, despite the smoke and fires, and located the last survivor underneath the rubble.

⑨ Very *Smelly* ANIMALS

The best advice is to steer clear of these stinky creatures, from the most famously smelly—the skunk— to the misleadingly named honey badger.

1. Skunk **2.** Sloth **3. Lesser anteater**

4. Striped polecat **5. Opossum** **6.** Pangolin

7. Honey badger **8.** Musk ox **9. Wolverine**

5 Facts ABOUT HUMMINGBIRDS

1. **Hummingbirds get their name because of the humming sound their wings make.**

2. They eat nectar from plants, hovering above them while beating their wings super-fast.

3. **They have the largest brain and heart compared to body size of any other bird, and one of the fastest beating hearts in the whole animal kingdom—about 1,200 beats per minute during flight.**

4. Hummingbirds are the only birds that can rotate their wings in a circle. This special ability means they can fly in all directions—even upside down!

5. **The bee hummingbird is the world's smallest bird. Males—which are smaller than females—measure just 2.25 inches (57 mm) including the beak and tail, and weigh 0.05 ounces (1.6 g).**

12 HUMMINGBIRDS with Interesting Names

1. Snow-capped hummingbird
2. **Green-crowned brilliant hummingbird**
3. Wine-throated hummingbird
4. **Green hermit hummingbird**
5. Marvellous spatuletail
6. **Calliope hummingbird**
7. Booted racket-tail hummingbird
8. **Ruby-topaz hummingbird**
9. Velvet-purple coronet
10. **Green-throated mango hummingbird**
11. Violet-crowned woodnymph
12. **Long-tailed hermit**

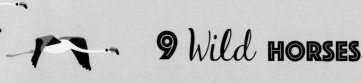

9 Wild HORSES

All of these horses run wild and free in different parts of the world. Strictly speaking, they're not truly wild but feral, because they are descended from domestic horses that escaped, were turned loose, or were reintroduced to the wild.

1. Przewalski's horses live in Russia and Mongolia. They were originally wild, but the population died out so that only domesticated Przewalski's horses were left. They were reintroduced to the wild in the 1990s.

2. The largest number of feral horses in the world lives in Australia, where they're known as brumbies. They're descended from herds introduced by settlers.

3. Dartmoor ponies roam free on Dartmoor, southwest England. They used to carry loads of tin from mines, and when the mines closed the ponies were turned loose.

4. Namib desert horses are probably the descendants of World War I cavalry horses.

5. Kaimanawa horses live in New Zealand. Horses were first introduced to New Zealand in 1814, and have been living there wild since the end of the 19th century.

6. Camargue horses are thought to be one of the oldest breeds in the world. They live in the marshy Camargue region of southern France. They are born black or brown, but as they get older their coats become completely white.

7. Misaki ponies run wild in the Mayazaki Province of Japan. At the end of the 17th century the ponies were used for farming and military work, but when they weren't needed they were left to run free.

8. Mustangs are the wild horses of the western United States, descended from horses brought to North America from Spain.

9. Pottoka ponies live in the Basque region of France and Spain.

13
Black-and-white Animals

1. **Giant panda**
2. Orca
3. **Zebra**
4. Malayan tapir
5. **Dalmatian dog**
6. Ring-tailed lemur
7. **Skunk**
8. Pied bat
9. **Giant leopard moth**

10. Californian king snake
11. **Penguin (all kinds—some have brightly colored crests just to show off!)**
12. Zebra longwing butterfly
13. **Black-and-white colobus monkey**

7

Facts About Orcas

....

1. **Orcas are the largest members of the dolphin family, up to 33 feet (10 m) long.**

2. They live in groups called pods, which can have up to 40 members.

3. **Orcas are very intelligent and make lots of different sounds to communicate with other members of their pod. Each pod has its own distinctive noises.**

4. Like bats, orcas use echolocation—they make noises that bounce off objects and give information about the objects' size, shape, and distance.

5. **Orcas are fearsome predators and hunt together as a pod. They catch and eat fish, penguins, seals, sea lions, squid, seabirds, and even whales.**

6. Orcas can swim up to 40 miles (65 km) a day and dive up to 1,640 feet (500 m) deep.

7. **They can live to be 100 years old.**

6 Animals with a NASTY Bite

1. Mosquitos can spread deadly diseases including malaria, which is transmitted when malaria-carrying mosquitos pass on a parasite in their bite. Malaria kills hundreds of thousands of people every year.

2. Fleas can carry the bacterium that causes plague. Today the disease can be treated with antibiotics.

3. Deer ticks can transmit bacteria that cause the very nasty Lyme disease.

4. Infected dogs, bats, foxes, raccoons, and skunks can spread the deadly disease rabies.

5. Tsetse flies can transmit Trypanosomiasis, also known as sleeping sickness, among other deadly diseases.

6. Cats can spread cat scratch disease when they bite or scratch if they're carrying a particular bacterium. The disease makes people sick but it's not deadly.

9 Animals from GREEK MYTHOLOGY

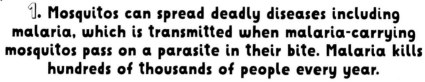

The Ancient Greeks told some amazing stories, populated by three-headed dogs, flying horses, and all sorts of hybrids.

1. The Echidna: part woman and part snake, who is the mother of all sorts of terrible Ancient Greek monsters.

2. Cerberus: three-headed dog.

3. Harpies: part woman, part bird.

4. Centaurs: half man, half horse.

5. Pegasus: flying horse.

6. The Sphinx: with the head of a human and the body of a lion.

7. The Mares of Diomedes: four man-eating horses owned by the giant Diomedes.

8. The Minotaur: part bull and part man.

9. Sea-goats: part goat, part fish.

12 RATTY *Facts*

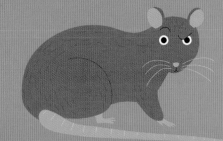

1. Rats are found all over the world. The brown rat and the house rat are the most common and have spread across the planet by stowing away on ships.

2. There are 51 known species of rat.

3. Rats stick together in groups called packs—new packs are formed when a male and female nest in an area that doesn't already contain a pack.

4. Most rats will eat almost anything—household trash, insects, snails, fish, birds, mammals . . . you name it, a rat will probably eat it.

5. There are vegetarian rats, including the Sulawesi white-tailed rat.

6. Whilst on their travels around the globe, brown and house rats have been responsible for the extinction of native species of small mammals, birds, and reptiles, especially on oceanic islands.

7. The brown and house rat have been implicated in the spread of 40 human diseases, including the bubonic plague.

8. Most rats can swim.

9. Rats are social creatures and like to be around other rats (and their human owners if they've been raised as a pet). They will show signs of loneliness if on their own for too long. They laugh when they're tickled!

10. Rats have excellent memories and can recognize faces they have seen before. They also have a very good sense of direction.

11. A rat's whiskers are very sensitive and send messages to the rat's brain that tell it about its environment—the whiskers act as extra eyes and ears.

12. Rats use their tails to help them balance, making them very good climbers.

5 SPIKY ANIMALS

1. Echidna—a spiky Australian marsupial.

2. Hedgehog—there are 17 kinds of hedgehog and all of them are prickly.

3. Porcupine—these are large rodents with long, sharp quills. There are different kinds found in Europe, Asia, and Africa ("old world" porcupines) and in North and South America ("new world" porcupines).

4. Sea urchin—spiny animals related to starfish.

5. Thorny devil—an Australian lizard with impressive spikes.

16 DINOSAURS

Around 700 different kinds of dinosaur have been discovered so far. They walked the Earth during the Mesozoic Era, also known as the Age of the Dinosaurs, which ended 65 million years ago (mya).

1. ALAMOSAURUS
69-foot-long (21-m-long) plant-eater that lived around 70–65 mya.

2. ALLOSAURUS
39-foot-long (12-m-long) carnivore that lived 156–144 mya.

3. ANKYLOSAURUS
Plant-eating armored dinosaur, 23 feet (7 m) long, that lived 74–67 mya.

4. BRACHIOSAURUS
100-foot-long (30-m-long) plant eater that lived 155–140 mya.

5. CERATOSAURUS
Meat-eating 20-foot-long (6-m-long) dinosaur that lived 150–144 mya.

6. COMPSOGNATHUS
Small (25.5 inches/65 cm) meat-eater that lived 145–140 mya.

7. DILOPHOSAURUS
Crested 20-foot-long (6-m-long) meat-eater that lived 190 mya.

8. EDMONTOSAURUS
Beaked plant-eater, 43 feet (13 m) long, that lived 76–65 mya.

9. GIGANOTOSAURUS
Carnivorous 41-foot-long (12.5-m-long) dinosaur that lived 112–90 mya.

10. MONOLOPHOSAURUS
Crested carnivore measuring 19 feet (5.7m) that lived 180–159 mya.

11. PARASAUROLOPHUS
38-foot-long (11.5-m-long) vegetarian duck-billed dinosaur with a backward-facing crest, that lived 76–74 mya.

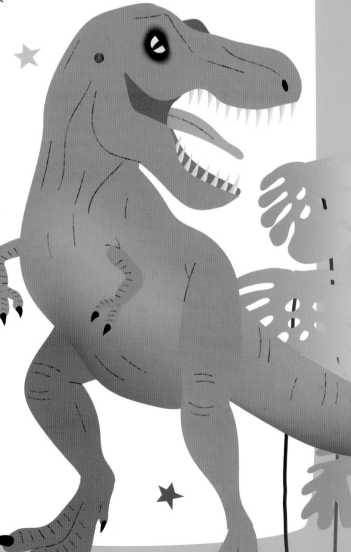

12. SPINOSAURUS
Huge (59 feet/18 m) fish-eating dinosaur with a sail on its back supported by long bones. Lived 95–70 mya.

13. STEGOSAURUS
Plant-eating armored 30-foot-long (9-m-long) dinosaur that lived 155–145 mya.

14. TRICERATOPS
30-foot-long (9-m-long), three-horned, herbivorous dinosaur that lived 68–66 mya.

15. TROODON
6.5-foot-long (2-m-long) meat-eater that lived 74–65 mya.

16. TYRANNOSAURUS REX
39-foot-long (12-m-long) meat-eater that lived 68–66 mya.

6 PREHISTORIC SHARKS

1. CLADOSELACHE
One of the earliest sharks from 400 million years ago.

2. HELICOPRIO
This shark's teeth were arranged in a spiral shape like a circular saw. It lived 290 million years ago.

3. HYBODUS
This shark had sharp teeth for biting and flat teeth for breaking open shells. It lived at the same time as the dinosaurs, 180 million years ago.

4. CRETOXYRHINA
Also lived at the same time as the dinosaurs, around 100 million years ago. It had seven rows of 2.75-inch-long (7-cm-long) teeth.

5. OTODUS
Thought to be a distant ancestor of today's great white shark, it lived around 55 million years ago.

6. MEGALODON
The biggest shark that ever lived, as far as we know. It was around 50 feet (15 m) long and lived until 2.6 million years ago.

17 Types of OWL

There are more than 200 different species of these beautiful, silent predators—here are just a few:

1. **Barn owl**   2. Barred owl   3. **Burrowing owl**
4. Eagle owl   5. **Elf owl**   6. Great gray owl   7. **Great horned owl**
8. Long-eared owl   9. **Little owl**   10. Northern hawk owl
11. **Saw-whet owl**   12. Short-eared owl   13. **Snowy owl**
14. Spectacled owl   15. **Spotted owl**   16. Tawny owl
17. **Western screech owl**

12 POPULAR Pets

What would we do without our furry, feathery, and scaly friends? Dogs are the most popular of all, but there are all sorts of pets to choose from.

1. **Dog**   2. Cat   3. **Goldfish (and other kinds of freshwater fish)**
4. Rabbit   5. **Guinea pig**   6. Hamster   7. **Gerbil**   8. Mouse
9. **Parrot, cockatiel, and budgie**   10. Snake
11. **Lizard**   12. Tropical fish

16

4
ENORMOUS
WHALES

1. **BLUE WHALE**—the biggest creature that's ever lived on Earth—up to 105 ft. (32 m) long, 180 tons

2. **FIN WHALE**—up to 85 ft. (26 m) long, 80 tons

3. **RIGHT WHALE** - up to 49 ft. (15 m) long, 65 tons

4. **SPERM WHALE** - up to 66 ft. (20 m) long, 50 tons

8
INCREDIBLE
Crustaceans

Crustaceans have been around since the Cambrian period, more than 485 million years ago. They're related to insects, and most of them live in water. They range in size from the huge American lobster, which can weigh 44 pounds (20 kg), and the Japanese spider crab, which has a leg span that can measure more than 11.5 feet (3.5 m), to teeny-tiny water fleas 0.01 inches (0.25 mm) long.

1. **Barnacle**
2. Crab
3. **Lobster**
4. Crayfish
5. **Krill**
6. Shrimp
7. **Water flea**
8. Woodlouse

28 Polar Animals

All of these animals live at the cold poles of our planet. Numbers 1 to 16 live in the Arctic in the frozen north, and numbers 17 to 28 live in the Antarctic in the icy south.

1. **Arctic fox** 2. Caribou 3. **Lemming** 4. Musk ox 5. **Polar bear**

6. Sea otter 7. **Arctic hare** 8. Snowshoe hare 9. **Orca** 10. Seal 11. **Walrus**

12. Narwhal 13. **Greenland shark** 14. Arctic wolf 15. **Puffin** 16. Snowy owl

17. **Emperor penguin** 18. King penguin 19. **Chinstrap penguin**

20. Antarctic minke whale 21. **Gray's beaked whale** 22. Orca

23. **Southern fur seal** 24. Leopard seal 25. **Southern elephant seal**

26. Wandering albatross 27. **Snow petrel** 28. Giant petrel

8 Animal Heroes *from* Wonderful Books

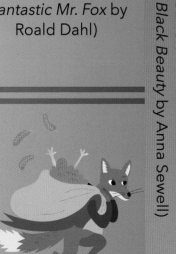

1

MR. FOX THE . . . FOX!
(*Fantastic Mr. Fox* by Roald Dahl)

2

BLACK BEAUTY THE HORSE
(*Black Beauty* by Anna Sewell)

3

CHARLOTTE THE SPIDER
(*Charlotte's Web* by E.B. White)

4

DESPEREAUX THE MOUSE
(*The Tale of Despereaux* by Kate DiCamillo)

5

HEDWIG THE OWL
(*Harry Potter* series by J.K. Rowling)

6

ASLAN THE LION
(*The Chronicles of Narnia* series by C.S. Lewis)

7

BABE THE PIG
(*The Sheep-Pig* by Dick King-Smith)

8

PERDITA AND PONGO THE DALMATIANS
(*101 Dalmatians* by Dodie Smith)

3 Amazon World Records

1. The world's smallest monkey, the pygmy marmoset.

2. The world's loudest land animal, the howler monkey.

3. The world's biggest eagle, the harpy eagle.

③ Animal *Ingredients* in Cosmetics

1. Ambergris, a black substance made in a sperm whale's digestive system, used in perfumes.

2. Fish scales are used in lipsticks and nail varnishes.

3. Cochineal, a red dye made from crushed beetles, used in various cosmetics as well as some foods.

10 Pink Animals

1. Amazon river dolphin, which lives only in the Amazon and Orinoco rivers in South America.

2. Axolotl, a type of salamander.

3. Dragon millipede, a small, bright pink millipede only discovered in 2007.

4. Flamingo, which is born with gray feathers but turns pink because of its diet of pink shrimp.

5. Orchid mantis, a type of praying mantis that's very hard to spot against pink orchid flowers.

6. Pink hairy squat lobster, in fact a type of crab that is 0.5 in. (1.2cm) long, pink to purple in color and covered in white hairs.

7. Pygmy seahorse, a tiny seahorse that blends in with its coral reef habitat.

8. Roseate skimmer, a type of dragonfly. Only the males are pink in color.

9. Hopkins rose nudibranch, a bright pink sea slug.

10. Kaputar pink slug, also shocking pink, is a slug that lives on land.

5 FACTS ABOUT Tree Frogs

1. There are over 800 species of tree frog, and they're found on every continent except Antarctica.

2. Tree frogs use pads on their toes to help them climb.

3. The smallest tree frog ever discovered is *Paedophryne amanuensis*, which lives in Papua New Guinea and is just 0.3 inches (7.7 mm) long. It's also the smallest known animal with a backbone.

4. Eighteen times bigger, at up to 5.5 inches (14 cm) long, is the white-lipped tree frog, the biggest kind of tree frog in the world.

5. The most poisonous animal in the world is a tree frog —the golden poison frog, which lives in the Colombian rainforest. It has just a milligram of poison on its skin, but that's enough to kill ten adult people. Emberá tribespeople sometimes put poison from the frog onto their blow darts when they go hunting.

9 ANIMALS Without Brains

If you thought all animals had brains, you'd be wrong. These sea creatures get by without doing any thinking at all.

1. Jellyfish   2. Sea anemone   3. Oyster

4. Sea cucumber   5. Sea sponge (yes, sponges are animals)

6. Coral (so are corals)   7. Sea urchin   8. Clam   9. Starfish

19 Breeds of CAT

1. **Abyssinian**
2. American shorthair
3. **Bengal**
4. Birman
5. **British shorthair**
6. Burmese
7. Devon rex
8. **Himalayan**
9. Maine coon
10. **Nebelung**
11. Norwegian forest
12. **Oriental shorthair**
13. Persian
14. **Ragdoll**
15. Russian blue
16. **Scottish fold**
17. Siamese
18. **Siberian**
19. Sphinx

16 Animals from New Zealand

New Zealand is made up of islands isolated in the Pacific Ocean. Some unusual creatures have evolved there—these animals aren't found anywhere else in the world.

1. **Chevron skink (a type of lizard)**
2. Hamilton's frog
3. **Hector's dolphin (the world's smallest dolphin)**
4. Hooker's sea lion
5. **Kakapo (a flightless parrot)**
6. Kea (another parrot, and the only alpine one in the world)
7. **Kiwi bird**
8. Lesser short-tailed bat
9. **Little blue penguin**
10. Maui dolphin
11. **Morepork owl**
12. New Zealand fantail (a type of bird)
13. **New Zealand fur seal**
14. Tuatara (a lizard-like reptile, a survivor from the age of the dinosaurs)
15. **Tui (a type of bird)**
16. Yellow-eyed penguin

3 Frightening FISH

1. GREAT WHITE SHARK

People are often afraid of sharks because they're enormous, fast, and have very sharp teeth, and the great white is probably the most feared of all. But it's worth bearing in mind that there are just a handful of fatal shark attacks on people per year, while people kill millions of sharks every year.

2. PIRANHA

Piranhas live in freshwater in South America. They sometimes bite off people's fingers and toes, and, very rarely, piranha attacks can be fatal. But usually these sharp-toothed fish prey on much smaller animals, and some are vegetarian.

3. STONEFISH

These warty-looking fish blend in with the rocky sea floor and can be tricky to spot. They have venomous spines which they raise when they're threatened, sometimes into the feet and legs of passing people. The venom is extremely painful and can kill.

6 Working DOGS

These furry companions are especially useful, and some of them are pets when they're not hard at work.

1. Herding dogs herd sheep and cattle. Border collies and Australian kelpies are two of the breeds that can be trained to be excellent sheep dogs.

2. Therapy dogs are taken to hospitals and retirement homes to cheer people up. All kinds of dogs can make good therapy dogs.

3. Sniffer dogs are trained to sniff out all sorts of things—bombs, illegal drugs, and even termites. Beagles, bloodhounds, spaniels, and German shepherd dogs are often trained as sniffer dogs.

4. Assistance dogs can be trained to help people with disabilities. Guide dogs for sight-impaired people are often Labradors.

5. In the past, sled dogs were used to transport people and supplies in snow-bound parts of the world. Today there are motorized sleds, but sled dogs are still used, and it's a popular sport too. Alaskan huskies are the most popular breed for sporting sled dogs.

6. Guard dogs guard buildings, and some guard other animals. The Hungarian sheepdog, or Komondor, looks a bit like a sheep, and guards the flock from predators.

How to Say "Quack-Quack!" in 8 different LANGUAGES

3. French coin coin

4. Italian ciarlatano-ciarlatano

1. Afrikaans kwak-kwak

2. Chinese guāguā

7. Serbian kva kva

5. Japanese gāgā

6. Russian krya krya

8. Turkish vakvak

10 WILD DOGS

All of these wild animals are related to domestic dogs—but are unlikely to want their tummies tickled. Dholes (wild dogs from southeast Asia), African wild dogs, and all three wolves are endangered.

1. **Dingo** 2. **Red fox** 3. **Golden jackal**
4. **African wild dog** 5. **Gray wolf**
6. **Maned wolf** 7. **Ethiopian wolf**
8. **Dhole** 9. **Coyote**
10. **Short-eared dog**

6
Facts about
Great Apes

. . . .

1. Humans are great apes, along with chimpanzees, bonobos, gorillas, and orangutans.

2. Our closest living relatives are chimpanzees and bonobos (which used to be called pygmy chimpanzees).

3. Chimps are omnivores—they eat plants and also hunt and kill other animals.

4. Orangutans and gorillas are mostly vegetarian—but orangutans have been known to kill and eat small primates.

5. Gorillas are the biggest great ape—they can weigh up to 440 pounds (200 kg).

6. Gorillas, orangutans, chimpanzees, and bonobos are all endangered, mainly due to habitat loss. Humans are the only great ape that isn't endangered.

3
ANIMAL Dads

1. Lots of different kinds of male frogs look after their young. One of the most devoted is the smooth guardian frog found in Borneo. It waits for its eggs to hatch then gives the tadpoles a piggyback to the nearest pool.

2. Male seahorses carry the eggs laid by the female seahorse inside a pouch until they hatch.

3. Female giant waterbugs glue their eggs to male giant waterbugs' backs. The males then carry the eggs around, keeping them clean and safe until they hatch.

7

JUMPING
Insects

· · · · · · · · · · · ·

Insects are a lot better at jumping than us puny humans. The highest recorded jump by an insect was a froghopper's 27.5 inches (70 cm) leap—which is pretty impressive because a froghopper is only around 2.4 inches (60 mm) long. It would be like you jumping to the top of a 35-story building. Fleas do even better, but jump horizontally rather than vertically—they can jump 200 times their body length.

1. **Froghopper**
2. Click beetle
3. **Leafhopper**
4. Cricket
5. **Flea**
6. Grasshopper
7. **Locust**

14

Types OF *Chicken*

· · · · · · · · · · · · · · ·

1. **Ancona**
2. Araucana
3. **Blue Andalusian**
4. Cochin
5. **Easter egger**
6. Frizzle
7. **Japanese bantam**
8. Jersey giant
9. **Orpington**
10. Plymouth Rock
11. **Rhode Island red**
12. Silkie
13. **Speckled Sussex**
14. White crested black Polish

5 Incredible Migrations

1. **Arctic terns have the longest migration of any animal—43,500 miles (70,000 km) from pole to pole.**

2. The monarch butterfly travels 2,980 miles (4,800 km) across North America. It takes them six months, but they only live for two months—each generation knows how to continue the journey.

3. **Humpback whales migrate from the Antarctic to warmer seas in the Pacific Ocean, a journey of around 3,100 miles (5,000 km).**

4. Globe-skimmer dragonflies have the longest insect migration, traveling 11,000 miles (17,700 km) following the monsoon around the Indian Ocean.

5. **Wildebeest on the Serengeti in eastern Africa begin a 620-mile (1,000-km) migration every year, the largest movement of land mammals in the world.**

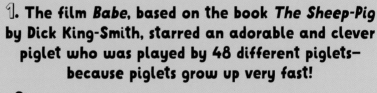

5 Animal Film Stars

1. **The film *Babe*, based on the book *The Sheep-Pig* by Dick King-Smith, starred an adorable and clever piglet who was played by 48 different piglets— because piglets grow up very fast!**

2. Hooch the crime-fighting dog was one of the heroes of the 1980s film *Turner and Hooch*, alongside the actor Tom Hanks. Hooch was played by Beasley the French mastiff.

3. **Actor Clint Eastwood starred in the 1979 film *Every Which Way But Loose* with an orangutan named Manis, who played Clyde.**

4. *Lassie Come Home* was the first film in a series starring a resourceful rough collie dog. Lassie was first played by a dog named Pal, then by Pal's descendants.

5. **Terry the terrier played Toto in *The Wizard of Oz*, starring Judy Garland.**

5 Absolutely ENORMOUS Animals

1. **The blue whale is the largest animal that has ever lived on Earth, including the dinosaurs. It can measure 105 feet (32 m) long and weigh 180 tons.**

2. African elephants are the biggest land animal in the world, at up to 7 tons in weight.

3. **The white rhinoceros can weigh up to 4 tons.**

4. Another African animal, the hippopotamus, can also weigh 4 tons.

5. **Giraffes weigh up to 1.4 tons, with the added bonus that they're the tallest animals in the world–up to 19.5 feet (5.8 m) is the tallest ever recorded.**

9 Proverbs about ANIMALS from AROUND the WORLD

Take heed of this wise advice.

1. **If you go to a donkey's house, don't talk about ears. (Jamaica)**

2. Don't insult the alligator until you've crossed the river. (Haiti)

3. **Don't count your chickens before they've hatched. (UK and USA)**

4. A frog in a well does not know the great sea. (Japan)

5. **Use your enemy's hand to catch a snake. (Iran)**

6. The fool who owns an ox is seldom recognized as a fool. (South Africa)

7. **A flea can trouble a lion more than a lion can trouble a flea. (Kenya)**

8. In a battle between elephants, the ants get squashed. (Thailand)

9. **If you want to keep camels, have a big enough door. (Afghanistan)**

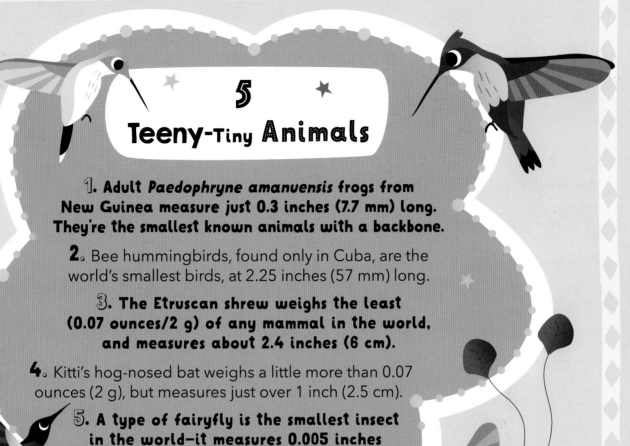

5
Teeny-Tiny Animals

1. Adult _Paedophryne amanuensis_ frogs from New Guinea measure just 0.3 inches (7.7 mm) long. They're the smallest known animals with a backbone.

2. Bee hummingbirds, found only in Cuba, are the world's smallest birds, at 2.25 inches (57 mm) long.

3. The Etruscan shrew weighs the least (0.07 ounces/2 g) of any mammal in the world, and measures about 2.4 inches (6 cm).

4. Kitti's hog-nosed bat weighs a little more than 0.07 ounces (2 g), but measures just over 1 inch (2.5 cm).

5. A type of fairyfly is the smallest insect in the world—it measures 0.005 inches (0.139 mm).

12 Tropical Fish

· ·

These are a few of the many beautiful fish that live in the world's tropical seas.

1. Angelfish   **2.** Butterfly fish   **3. Cardinal fish**   **4.** Clownfish
5. Damselfish   **6.** Goby   **7. Grouper**   **8.** Mandarin fish
9. Parrotfish   **10.** Surgeonfish   **11. Triggerfish**   **12.** Wrasse

21

BIRDS of Paradise

There are more than 30 kinds of birds of paradise, all of which are found in New Guinea and its surrounding islands, and Australia. They are often brightly colored, with ruffs around their necks or long, dangly feathers that are known as wires or streamers. Many perform elaborate mating dances. Here are some of the loveliest names:

1. **Carola's parotia**
2. Black sicklebill
3. **Ribbon-tailed astrapia**
4. Bronze parotia
5. **Trumpet manucode**
6. Goldie's bird-of-paradise
7. **Magnificent riflebird**
8. Superb bird-of-paradise
9. **Paradise riflebird**
10. Paradise crow

4
EXTRAORDINARY
Bird Displays

These birds have
something to crow about!

2. Andean flamingos strut
about in a group mating dance,
turning their heads sharply
like tango dancers.

**1. Peacocks, or male
peafowls, are the most
famous bird show-offs. They
raise their extraordinary tail
feathers into a beautiful fan
to impress a mate.**

3. To impress a mate, male magnificent frigatebirds inflate their throat sacs into a huge red balloon, then clack their beaks to make a drumming sound on the sac.

4. Birds of paradise have all sorts of amazing mating displays. The Vogelkop superb bird-of-paradise has a vivid turquoise breast cover and a deep black cape.

4 ANIMAL SUPERHEROES

POW! POW!

1. Rocket Raccoon, Marvel comics superhero and one of the Guardians of the Galaxy.

2. Krypto the Superdog, Superman's pet dog, who had his own TV series in the US.

3. Teenage Mutant Ninja Turtles, named after Italian Renaissance artists Donatello, Michelangelo, Leonardo, and Raphael.

4. Danger Mouse, superhero star of the British TV animation series, who saves the world with his hamster sidekick Penfold.

16 Clever Crows

There are lots of crows—more than 40 different kinds—and they are found in most parts of the world. Even though their brains are less than the size of a walnut, they are remarkably clever animals.

1. **Australian raven**
2. Brown-headed crow
3. **Cape crow**
4. Carrion crow
5. **Common raven**
6. Fan-tailed raven
7. **Fish crow**
8. Indian jungle crow
9. **Jamaican crow**
10. Little raven
11. **Pied crow**
12. Rook
13. **Somali crow**
14. Violet crow
15. **White-billed crow**
16. White-necked raven

4 Deadly Snakes

These four snakes are the world's deadliest—they live near people and are aggressive, a combination that's lethal to thousands of people every year.

1. **Saw-scaled viper**
2. Indian cobra
3. **Common krait**
4. Russell's viper

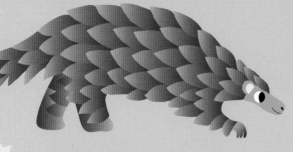

4 *Armored* ANIMALS

1. Armadillos have shells made of bony plates covered in a layer of keratin, the same stuff your nails and hair are made of.

2. Pangolins, found in Africa and Asia, have scales made of keratin that protect them from predators.

3. Arapaimas are huge fish found in the Amazon. They are covered in three layers of tough scales that not even piranhas can bite through.

4. All beetles are covered in a hard shell, but ironclad beetles, from the US and Mexico, are the toughest of the lot.

4 Animals with Tusks

Tusks are modified teeth that stick out of an animal's mouth, looking impressive and a bit alarming.

1. Narwhal—a type of whale with perhaps the most impressive tusk of all, a single spiral tusk that can measure nearly 10 feet (3 m) long.

2. Elephants use their giant tusks for digging, lifting, and stripping bark from trees.

3. Walruses sometimes use their 3-foot-long (1-m-long) tusks to haul themselves out of the water and make holes in ice.

4. Warthogs have two pairs of tusks which help them root for food.

13 BLUE ANIMALS

1. Blue iguana
2. Little blue heron
3. Moon jellyfish
4. Blue poison dart frog
5. Blue starfish
6. Blue morpho butterfly
7. Carpathian blue slug
8. Blue-headed agama lizard
9. Steel-blue ladybird
10. Hyacinth macaw
11. Blue dacnis (a bird)
12. Blue-footed booby (another bird)
13. Blue dasher dragonfly

6
BIRDS OF PREY

Birds of prey are also known as raptors. They have super-keen eyesight, sharp talons, a hooked beak for tearing flesh, and are very fast indeed.

1. ANDEAN CONDOR
The world's largest bird of prey, with a wingspan of up to 11 feet (3.3 m), found in South America.

2. BALD EAGLE
Found in North America and the national emblem of the USA, bald eagles aren't bald at all but have white-feathered heads.

3. BARN OWL
Owls are the only birds of prey that hunt when the sun goes down. Barn owls are the most widely distributed kind.

4. COMMON BUZZARD
Widespread in Europe and some of Asia.

5. GOLDEN EAGLE
Found in Europe, Asia, and North America.

6. PEREGRINE FALCON
Peregrine falcons are among the world's most common birds of prey and live on all continents except Antarctica.

10 MARINE Mammals

Marine mammals all live in or by the sea, and they all rely on it to live. But other than that, they're quite a diverse bunch. The first three on the list are known as cetaceans, the second three are pinnipeds, the next two are sirenians, and finally the last two—which you might not have realized were classed as marine mammals at all—are known as marine fissipeds.

1. Whales
2. Dolphins
3. Porpoises
4. Seals
5. Sea lions
6. Walruses
7. Manatees
8. Dugongs
9. Polar bears
10. Sea otters

10 *Tricks* You Can TEACH *your* Cat

Cats aren't famous for doing tricks, but with patience, kindness, and lots of cat treats, you can teach them all sorts of tricks. Train your cat in short bursts and stop before they get bored. Try these:

1. Sit
2. Stay
3. Lie down
4. Stand up
5. Fetch a toy
6. Wave
7. Shake paws
8. Spin around
9. Jump through a hoop
10. Roll over

8 FACTS About DOLPHINS and PORPOISES

1. Dolphins are social animals and live in groups called pods, which usually have between two and thirty members.

2. Dolphins communicate with each other using clicks, squeaks, pops, and whistling noises.

3. Most dolphins are sea creatures, but there are four kinds of river dolphin.

4. Orcas are the biggest dolphins of the lot. They can weigh up to 11 tons, and the fin on their backs can measure 6.5 feet (2 m) long. They're the only dolphins that live in the Arctic and waters of the Antarctic.

5. There are seven kinds of porpoise, which are smaller than dolphins, with a rounded snout and differently shaped teeth.

6. The speediest porpoise is the Dall's, which can swim at over 31 mph (50 km/h).

7. The smallest species of dolphin is the Maui's dolphin, found off the coast of New Zealand. It's in danger of extinction.

8. The smallest species of porpoise is also the most endangered—vaquita porpoises live off the coast of Mexico.

11 ORANGE Animals

1. **Eastern newt** (in its juvenile stage)
2. Goldfish
3. **Clownfish**
4. Monarch butterfly
5. **Red fox**
6. Madagascar fody (bird)
7. **Orangutan**
8. Corn snake
9. **Orange sea star**
10. Tiger
11. **King baboon spider**

10 Curiously Named BATS

There are more than 1,000 different kinds of bat, so this is a very small but oddly named sample.

1. **GHOST BAT:** this bat looks ghostly because it has white fur.

2. **BANANA BAT:** a long-snouted bat often found in the banana plantations of western Mexico.

3. **PALE SPEAR-NOSED BAT:** from Central and South America, this bat does indeed have a very pointy nose.

4. **MONKEY-FACED BAT:** there are different kinds of these lovely fruit bats, which all come from Papua New Guinea and surrounding islands. Many are endangered.

5. **HAMMER-HEADED BAT:** a fruit bat and the largest bat in Africa. Males have enormous, hammer-like heads.

6. **SUCKER-FOOTED BAT:** these bats from Madagascar pull themselves along with a gluey substance they produce from their wings and legs. People used to think they were using suckers.

7. **MEDITERRANEAN HORSESHOE BAT:** this bat's nose is shaped very much like a horseshoe.

8. **TUBE-NOSED FRUIT BAT:** there are lots of kinds of tube-nosed bat, which do indeed have tube-shaped nostrils.

9. **BUMBLEBEE BAT:** also known as Kitti's hog-nosed bat, this is the smallest bat in the world. It is not much bigger than a bumblebee at just over 1 inch (25 mm) long and 0.07 ounces (2 g) in weight.

10. **WRINKLE-FACED BAT:** also known as "old man bat" where it lives in Central America and Mexico.

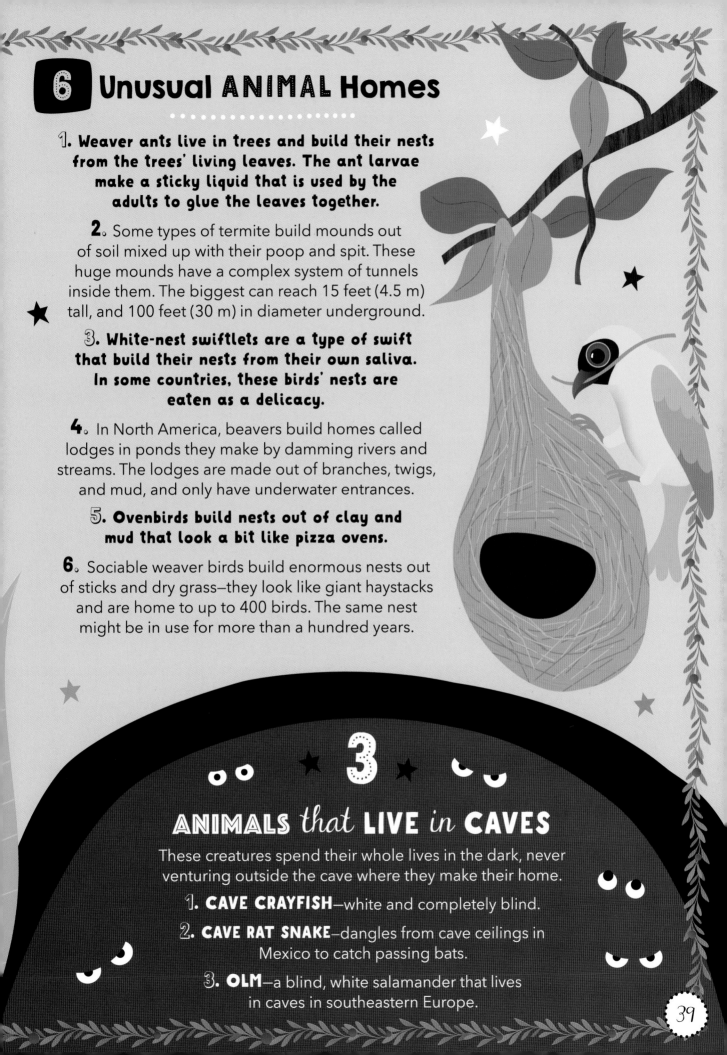

6 Unusual ANIMAL Homes

1. Weaver ants live in trees and build their nests from the trees' living leaves. The ant larvae make a sticky liquid that is used by the adults to glue the leaves together.

2. Some types of termite build mounds out of soil mixed up with their poop and spit. These huge mounds have a complex system of tunnels inside them. The biggest can reach 15 feet (4.5 m) tall, and 100 feet (30 m) in diameter underground.

3. White-nest swiftlets are a type of swift that build their nests from their own saliva. In some countries, these birds' nests are eaten as a delicacy.

4. In North America, beavers build homes called lodges in ponds they make by damming rivers and streams. The lodges are made out of branches, twigs, and mud, and only have underwater entrances.

5. Ovenbirds build nests out of clay and mud that look a bit like pizza ovens.

6. Sociable weaver birds build enormous nests out of sticks and dry grass—they look like giant haystacks and are home to up to 400 birds. The same nest might be in use for more than a hundred years.

3
ANIMALS that LIVE in CAVES

These creatures spend their whole lives in the dark, never venturing outside the cave where they make their home.

1. **CAVE CRAYFISH**—white and completely blind.

2. **CAVE RAT SNAKE**—dangles from cave ceilings in Mexico to catch passing bats.

3. **OLM**—a blind, white salamander that lives in caves in southeastern Europe.

7 Things TO DO with Dung

1. Dry animal dung is often used as fuel—cow, buffalo, sheep, and camel dung all burn well.

2. Paper can be made from the dung of vegetarian animals that eat a lot of fiber, including elephants, pandas, cows, horses, donkeys, and moose.

3. Camel dung has been eaten as a cure for the disease dysentery. Apparently, it's only effective if the dung is eaten when it's fresh!

4. Moose droppings are made into souvenirs in North America. Moose-dung gifts include mobiles and earrings.

5. Bat droppings contains a lot of potassium nitrate, and until the World War I they were used to make gunpowder and other explosives.

6. Bird poop—known as guano—has often been used as fertilizer in the past, and it's making a comeback because it's natural and environment-friendly.

7. The ingredients in nightingale guano are supposed to be especially good for the skin and are used in facials.

13 Marsupials

Marsupials are a group of mammals that carry their babies in a pouch. They live in Australia, South America, Central America, and North America, and there are more than 250 different kinds, including these beauties:

1. Marsupial mouse
2. Opossum
3. Bandicoot
4. Quokka
5. Glider
6. Potoroo
7. Kangaroo
8. Wallaby
9. Koala
10. Bilby
11. Tasmanian devil
12. Marsupial mole
13. Wombat

9 Creepy Crawlies that Aren't INSECTS

The terms "creepy crawlies" and "minibeasts" are sometimes used to include spiders, worms, snails, and insects. Insects are six-legged creatures with two antennae, and a body that comes in three parts— and all of these little creatures are definitely not insects.

1. **Centipedes—lots of legs (some have more than 350), one pair per body segment. They are fast-moving and catch and kill small creatures to eat.**

2. Millipede—even more legs than centipedes—there is one millipede that has 750! Unlike centipedes, millipedes move slowly and are vegetarians.

3. **Earthworms—no legs at all, slither around in soil all over the world.**

4. Scorpion—eight legs, two pincers, and a sting in their tail for killing their prey, which might be lizards, spiders, or mice.

5. **Spiders—eight legs and up to eight eyes.**

6. Ticks— related to spiders and scorpions, adult ticks have eight legs.

7. **Snails—no legs but four antennae, a shell keeps them damp and protected.**

8. Slugs—no legs, no shell (they have to hide underground to keep damp and safe) and four antennae.

9. **Woodlice—more closely related to shrimp and crabs than to insects, woodlice have 14 legs.**

4 Very Fast Animals

1. **Fastest animal: the peregrine falcon is the fastest animal in the world. It can fly at speeds of more than 200 miles per hour (320 km/h) when it dives to catch prey.**

2. Fastest land animal: the cheetah can run at 70 miles per hour (112 km/h) for short bursts.

3. **Fastest land animal over a long distance: the pronghorn antelope can run at 60 miles per hour (98 km/h) for long periods.**

4. Fastest fish: the black marlin is the world's fastest fish, swimming at the speeds of 80 miles per hour (129 km/h)—faster than a cheetah can run!

7 Zodiac ANIMALS

. . . .

1. **Aries, the ram**
2. Taurus, the bull
3. **Cancer, the crab**
4. Leo, the lion
5. **Scorpio, the scorpion**
6. Capricorn, the goat
7. **Pisces, the fish**

12 KINDS OF MONGOOSE

There are more than 30 different kinds of this small, meat-eating mammal, found mainly in Africa, but also in Asia and southern Europe. Here is a small selection.

1. **Banded mongoose**
2. Black mongoose
3. **Collared mongoose**
4. Gambian mongoose
5. **Egyptian mongoose**
6. Indian gray mongoose
7. **Long-nosed mongoose**
8. Marsh mongoose
9. **Meerkat**
10. Slender mongoose
11. **White-tailed mongoose**
12. Yellow mongoose

3 WARRIOR Animals

Soldiers have charged into battle mounted on . . .

1. **HORSES**—the horse-mounted cavalry was an important part of many armies more than a hundred years ago. In Europe, armored knights rode horses, and so did samurai warriors in Japan.

2. **CAMELS**—in desert warfare in the Middle East, armies often fought from the backs of camels.

3. **ELEPHANTS**—terrifying war elephants were used to charge at the enemy in battles in Asia and Europe.

3 FASTEST Birds Flying HORIZONTALLY

The peregrine falcon achieves its record-breaking speed by flying high up and then plummeting downward. Golden eagles and other birds of prey can go very fast in a vertical dive, too. But what about birds that fly along horizontally?

1. **Spine-tailed swift: 106 miles per hour (171 km/h)**

2. Frigate bird: 95 miles per hour (153 km/h)

3. **Spur-winged goose: 88 miles per hour (142 km/h)**

4 Prehistoric PREDATORS

1. **Megalodon was the biggest shark that ever lived, reaching around 50 feet (15 m) long. It died out 2.6 million years ago.**

2. Andrewsarchus is the largest meat-eating mammal that's ever lived, as far as we know. It could measure 20 feet (6 m) long and 6.5 feet (2 m) tall. It died out 35 million years ago.

3. **Smilodon was a saber-toothed cat with two extra-long teeth. It died out 10,000 years ago.**

4. Sarcosuchus was a massive crocodile, up to 30 feet (9 m) long and 3.5 tons in weight. It lived until 112 million years ago.

7 BIZARRE ANIMAL WORLD RECORDS

· · · · · · · · · · · · · · · · · ·

1. Most basketball slam dunks in one minute by a rabbit: the proud holder of this record is Bini the bunny, who achieved seven dunks.

2. The highest-ranking sheep was Lance Corporal Derby XXX, a member of the British Armed Forces, who was promoted to lance corporal from the rank of private in 2015.

3. Ninja the goat walked across a human bridge in 9.4 seconds to become the world-record holder in 2017.

4. Zac the macaw holds the world record for most canned drinks opened by a parrot in one minute (he managed to open 35).

5. The dog world record for popping 100 balloons is held by Toby the whippet, who popped 100 balloons in 36.53 seconds.

6. Caspa the llama holds the record for the highest bar jump cleared by a llama—3.71 feet (1.13 m).

7. In 2019, 1,048 alpacas came together in Juliaca, Peru, to set the world record for the largest alpaca parade.

8 Marvelous Monkeys

1. Howler monkey: one of the world's loudest animals, with a call that can be heard about 3 miles (5 km) away.

2. Burmese sneezing monkey: this monkey sneezes when it rains.

3. Golden snub-nosed monkey: an extremely furry monkey with beige fur and a blue face.

4. Bald uakari monkey: a red-faced Japanese monkey that sounds like a human when it laughs.

5. Pygmy marmoset: the world's smallest monkey, just over 3.5 ounces (100 g) in weight.

6. Mandrill: the world's biggest monkey, up to 100 pounds (45 kg) in weight, with a red-striped face and a blue bottom.

7. Gelada: communicates to other geladas with complex vocal sounds and lip-smacks.

8. Pata monkey: the fastest monkey, which can scoot along at 34 miles per hour (55 km/h).

9 ANIMALS with Powerful BITES

The force of a bite can be measured in kilopascals. The force of a human bite is around 1,117 kilopascals, which is absolutely pathetic compared to these fearsome chompers.

1. **Nile crocodile: 34,474 kilopascals**
2. Saltwater crocodile: 25,511 kilopascals
3. **American alligator: 15,272 kilopascals**
4. Hippo: 12,410 kilopascals
5. **Jaguar: 10,342 kilopascals**
6. Bull shark: 9,308 kilopascal
7. **Gorilla: 8,963 kilopascals**
8. Polar bear: 8,274 kilopascals
9. **Grizzly bear: 7,998 kilopascals**

6 Marvelous Monkey Facts

1. **Monkeys are primates, a group that also includes apes (e.g. gorillas and chimps) and prosimians (e.g. lemurs and tarsiers).**

2. There are more than 260 different kinds of monkey.

3. **Some monkeys, including howler monkeys and spider monkeys, have prehensile tails—tails that can grip on to branches and are used as an extra limb.**

4. Almost all wild monkeys live in South and Central America, Africa, and Asia. There's one monkey that lives in Europe —Barbary macaques live on the island of Gibraltar just off the coast of Spain.

5. **Monkeys are intelligent—and capuchin monkeys are some of the smartest. They use a flat rock as an anvil and another as a nutcracker, and they rub themselves with crushed-up millipedes to ward off mosquito bites.**

6. Monkeys are social animals and regularly groom one another's fur.

7 Narwhal FACTS

1. Narwhals are a type of whale found in Arctic seas and rivers.

2. They travel in groups and hunt fish and other sea creatures.

3. A narwhal's spiral "horn" is a tusk—a modified tooth that can grow as much as 10 feet (3 m) long.

4. Only male narwhals have long tusks —female narwhals sometimes grow tusks, but they are much shorter.

5. The narwhal's horn has earned it the nickname "unicorn of the sea."

6. Narwhals can grow up to 20 feet (6 m) long and weigh up to 1.5 tons.

7. They can stay underwater for up to 25 minutes without coming up for air, and reach depths of 1.1 miles (1.8 km).

7 Underground Animals

Lots of animals make their homes underground, safe from predators and sheltered from bad weather. As well as these burrowing mammals, there are different kinds of mole, insect, and snake that live underground, and there's even a burrowing owl.

1. ARMADILLO
There are 20 kinds, 19 of which live in South America and one in the United States. Most kinds dig burrows with their long, sharp claws, and sleep in them for up to 16 hours a day.

2. EUROPEAN BADGER
Found throughout Europe, these black-and-white animals dig networks of tunnels called setts. Fifteen or more badgers might live in a single sett.

8 FAMOUS PEOPLE'S Pets

1. The surrealist artist Salvador Dali had a pet ocelot—a type of wild cat —called Boubou, and a pet anteater.

2. Lord Byron, the English poet, had a pet wolf named Lyon and a bear that he brought with him when he went to Cambridge University.

3. US president Andrew Jackson had a pet parrot named Polly that swore in English and Spanish.

4. Another US president, Calvin Coolidge, had a pet pygmy hippo named William Johnson Hippopotamus.

5. Gérard de Nerval was a French poet who walked his pet lobster, Thibault, in the parks of Paris.

6. The artist Frida Kahlo had a pet deer.

7. Astronomer Tycho Brahe owned a pet moose.

8. Napoleon Bonaparte's wife, Josephine, was very fond of her pet orangutan, named Rose.

3. CHIPMUNK
Most chipmunk species live in North America (and one lives in northern Russia). Chipmunks build shallow burrows to hide in during the day, and much deeper ones where they nest and store food.

4. GROUNDHOG
Groundhogs live in North America and dig their burrows up to 3 feet (1 m) deep. A groundhog burrow is usually home to one animal and its young, and sometimes very small groups.

5. MEERKAT
Meerkats live in southern Africa in groups of up to about 50. Their burrows can be 16.5 feet (5 m) long and 6.5 feet (2 m) deep. During the day, one or more meerkats stand sentinel, looking out for danger.

6. PLATYPUS
This strange Australian mammal digs burrows in riverbanks.

7. RED FOX
Red foxes are medium-sized dog relatives that are widespread throughout the northern half of the world. They dig underground dens

3 ANIMAL Transformations

. . . .

These animals change dramatically as part of their life cycle.

1. Butterflies lay eggs, which hatch into caterpillars. Each caterpillar becomes a chrysalis with a hard casing around it. Eventually, an adult butterfly emerges from the chrysalis.

2. Dragonflies lay eggs near or in water, which hatch into nymphs. Eventually, after months or even years, the nymphs crawl out of the water and change into dragonflies.

3. Frogs lay eggs in a pond. The eggs hatch into tadpoles, which turn into froglets. Gradually, a froglet's tail shrinks, the legs grow, and finally it becomes an adult frog.

7 CRITICALLY Endangered *Animals*

1. Amur leopard: there are fewer than 30 of these big cats left in the wild because they've been hunted for their beautiful spotted fur. They live in southeastern Russia and northern China.

2. Javan rhino: the most endangered of the five kinds of rhino, there are fewer than 70 left in Ujung Kulon National Park in Java, Indonesia.

3. Black rhino: 98 percent of the population was wiped out in the 20th century because they were widely hunted as trophies and for their horns. There are now more than 5,000 black rhinos in the wild, twice the number in 1995, but they are still critically endangered.

4. Bornean orangutan: this ape's habitat on the island of Borneo is less than half what it was 20 years ago, because the forest has been cleared for palm oil plantations. About 100,000 Bornean orangutans remain in the wild.

5. Sunda pangolin: one of four Asian species of pangolin, which are still hunted for their scales.

6. Malayan tiger: found on the Malay Peninsula and southern Thailand, there are fewer than 400 of these animals left in the wild.

7. Hawksbill turtle: these turtles have been hunted for their colorful, patterned shells.

9 Colorful Parrots

Parrots are famous for their bright colors. Here are a few of the brightest.

1. **Scarlet macaw**
2. Sun parakeet
3. **Eclectus parrot**
4. Lilac-crowned Amazon parrot
5. **Rose-breasted cockatoo**
6. Blue-and-gold macaw
7. **Hyacinth macaw**
8. Blue-crowned parakeet
9. **Greenwing macaw**

7 ANIMALS SAVED from the Brink of Extinction

1. **Bald eagle: in the 1960s there were fewer than 500 of these birds in the United States. Today, there are more than 14,000 breeding pairs.**

2. Rodrigues fruit bat: at one point there were fewer than 100 of these bats left, but now they number more than 25,000.

3. **Blue iguana: found only on Grand Cayman Island in the Caribbean, there were just 12 blue iguanas left by 2002. A breeding program has meant that there are more than 600 living in protected areas on the island today.**

4. Snow leopard: conservation has meant that since 2017 these beautiful big cats are no longer classed as "endangered"—although they still need help to make their population stable.

5. **Mauritius kestrel: in 1974 there were only four of these birds of prey in the wild. Today there are about 400, thanks to conservation efforts.**

6. Giant panda: protection for this bear and the bamboo it eats has meant that its status is now "vulnerable" rather than "endangered."

7. **American alligator: in the middle of the 20th century, American alligators had been hunted almost to extinction. Thanks to efforts to protect them and their habitat, there are now more than 5 million.**

10
Ancient Egyptian Animal Mummies

1. **Crocodile** 2. Baboon
3. **Ibis** 4. Fish 5. **Snake**
6. Cat 7. **Dog** 8. Jackal
9. Falcon 10. **Bull**

7 CREATURES that Eat their Mate

The black widow spider gets its name because the female eats the male, but spiders aren't the only creatures who eat after mating.

1. **Black widow spider** 2. Jumping spider
3. **Tarantula** 4. Golden orb spider 5. **Praying mantis**
6. Green anaconda (a huge, constricting snake from South America)
7. **Several different kinds of octopus**

7 Facts about Crocodiles, ALLIGATORS, and Caimans

1. **Crocodiles live in the tropical regions of Africa, Asia, Australia, and the Americas.**

2. Crocodiles belong to the same big family group as alligators, caimans, and the gharial.

3. **Caimans are smaller than crocodiles and live in the Americas.**

4. **Gharials live in the Indian subcontinent and have nubby noses.**

5. Saltwater crocodiles are the world's biggest reptiles. They can measure more than 20 feet (6 m) long and can weigh more than a ton.

6. **The Nile crocodile has the strongest bite of any animal in the world.**

7. **It's tricky to tell the difference between crocs and alligators—alligators have U-shaped snouts, while a crocodile's is V-shaped.**

6 Facts about BEETLES

1. One out of every four living things on Earth (including plants) is a beetle—the largest group of living organisms on the planet. There are around 400,000 species, living almost everywhere on Earth, apart from the frozen poles.

2. Beetles hatch from eggs, spend most of their lives as larvae (grubs), then develop a pupa (hard outer casing) and eventually change into adult insects, like butterflies do.

3. Beetles have a tough external skeleton and two sets of wings, one of which is hard and acts as a casing to protect the other set of wings.

4. There are beetles that eat carpet, wood, clothing, flour, chocolate, grain, dung, animal hide, and even flesh. Museums use flesh-eating beetles (nicknamed "museum bugs") to clean the skeletons of new specimens.

5. The smallest beetle is the fringed ant beetle, Nanosella fungi, at 0.01 inches (0.25 mm) in length.

6. The Titan beetle, Titanus giganteus, from South America is the longest, with a body length of up to 8 inches (20 cm).

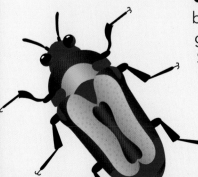

6 BEAUTIFUL BEETLES

1. Jewel beetle from Thailand: shiny and multicolored with a golden band around the middle.

2. Christmas beetle from Australia: brilliant green, named because there are lot of them around Christmastime.

3. Flower beetle from tropical regions of Africa: iridescent green, red, or purple colors.

4. Rainbow shield beetle from Mozambique, Tanzania, and Cameroon: dazzling metallic colors.

5. Picasso bug from sub-Saharan and northeastern Africa: beautiful, colorful geometric patterns.

6. Frog-legged leaf beetle from Thailand and Malaysia: green and gold metallic colors. Male beetles have huge hind legs like a frog's.

5 ANIMAL
Crowds

1. About 20 million Mexican free-tailed bats roost in a cave in Texas, USA, the largest colony of bats in the world.

2. Atlantic herring get together in enormous shoals of hundreds of millions of individual fish.

3. Honeybee colonies can include tens of thousands of individual bees—up to about 80,000.

4. You might have seen starlings mass together in a huge flock of 100,000 or more, known as a murmuration. They swoop and dive together before roosting at night, making dramatic patterns in the sky.

5. Red-billed queleas are the most numerous birds in the world and form flocks of many millions of birds as they fly across the African savanna.

5 ANIMALS
that BLEND with their SURROUNDINGS

1. Katydids look like leaves—different kinds look like part of a leaf, a whole leaf, a green leaf, a dead leaf, leaves with bird poop on them, and diseased leaves.

2. The leafy seadragon is a type of fish similar to a seahorse that looks like fronds of seaweed.

8 FACTS ABOUT Otters

1. There are 13 different species of otter—most live in freshwater rivers and lakes but some are sea otters. They live on every continent except Australia and Antarctica.

2. Otters have webbed feet and tails that act like rudders for steering.

3. An otter can close its nostrils and ears when swimming underwater.

4. A bit like dogs, an otter can tell a lot about another otter by sniffing its dung—how old it is, and whether it's male or female.

5. Otters have very thick fur in two layers, which traps air next to the animals' skin to keep them warm and dry and help them float. Otter pups have so much air trapped in their fur that they can't dive!

6. Otters are tool-users—they use stones to crack open shellfish, and store the stones in their armpits to use later!

7. Otters love to play and often create mud slides for themselves on riverbanks.

8. Sea otters loop themselves in kelp so they don't float away while they're taking a nap. Sometimes they intertwine their feet with another sea otter, so that they stay together.

3. The orchid mantis (tropical forests of Southeast Asia) is a praying mantis that attracts prey by looking like a beautiful orchid flower.

4. Giant geometer moth caterpillars look like sticks, and smell like them too because they absorb the scent chemicals in the plants they eat.

5. Stick insects look like sticks, obviously, and some kinds look like leaves. They sometimes sway to mimic a stick or leaf moving in the breeze.

4 Animals *that* Pretend *to be* **SOMETHING ELSE**

1. The harmless red milk snake mimics the colors of the venomous coral snake to discourage predators.

2. South American owl butterflies have large round spots on their wings that look like owl eyes to make predators think they are facing a larger, more dangerous animal.

3. Australia's death's head spider (named because its markings look a bit like a skull), is also known as the bird dropping spider. It hides from hungry birds by mimicking a blob of bird poop.

4. The hawkmoth caterpillar mimics the venomous pit viper snake to ward off attackers. It disguises itself by puffing out the front of its body. Two eyelike spots, fake scales, and a snakelike pose complete the transformation.

4 Animals **that** Sound LIKE Something **Else**

1. The crafty African fork-tailed drongo bird mimics warning calls made by meerkats and other animals when danger is approaching. As they flee, the drongo swoops in to steal their food.

2. The male lyrebird can mimic almost any sound—from mechanical manmade noises to the songs and calls of other creatures —in order to impress female lyrebirds.

3. Margay wildcats do an impression of the tiny pied tamarin monkey's call. Other pied tamarin monkeys come to see what's going on, then the margay pounces.

4. North American walnut sphinx moth caterpillars make a whistle like a bird's alarm call to frighten off predators.

4 Animals *that* PLAY DEAD

This is a good trick, whether you're avoiding a predator or catching your prey.

1. American opossums pretend to be dead and also produce horrible-smelling slime so that predators don't eat them.

2. Hognose snakes pretend to thrash as if they're dying, then lie still and make a terrible smell.

3. Leaf litter frogs play dead by lying on their backs with their eyes closed and their arms and legs thrown back.

4. Livingston's cichlid, a type of fish, pretends to be dead and floats to the bottom of the lake, then grabs and eats any smaller creatures that come to feed on it.

FACTS
ABOUT Tigers

1. Tigers are the world's biggest big cats, weighing up to 800 pounds (360 kg) and measuring more than 10 feet (3 m) long. Their tails can measure over 3 feet (1 m) long.

2. They eat only meat and usually prey on large mammals, including deer, buffalo, and antelope.

3. No two tigers have the same pattern of stripes.

4. Running at full speed, a tiger can reach 40 miles per hour (65 km/h).

5. Unlike most cats, tigers like water and are good swimmers.

6. There are five subspecies of tiger in the world today: Bengal, South China, Indochinese, Sumatran, and Siberian.

7. Hunting and habitat loss have meant that tigers now roam an area less than one-tenth the size it was 100 years ago.

8. Tiger numbers are rising because of conservation efforts. There are now around 3,900 tigers in the world, but they still need protection as much as ever.

10 VERY
Long SNAKES

. . . .

1. Titanoboa (now extinct, it was the longest snake that ever lived)–up to 49 feet (15 m)

2. Reticulated python–up to 28 feet (8.5 m)

3. Amethystine python–up to 28 feet (8.5 m)

4. Burmese python–up to 25 feet (7.6 m)

5. African rock python–up to 24.5 feet (7.5 m)

6. Green anaconda–up to 23 feet (7 m) (also the world's heaviest snake)

7. Indian python–21 feet (6.4 m)

8. King cobra–18.7 feet (5.7 m) (the world's longest venomous snake)

9. Black mamba–14 feet (4.3 m)

10. Boa constrictor–14 feet (4.3 m)

12 Egg-laying Animals that AREN'T BIRDS

1. **There are a few mammals, called monotremes, that lay eggs—the four species of echidna and the duck-billed platypus**

2. Snails

3. **Fish (most lay eggs but some give birth to live babies)**

4. Snakes (all boas and some vipers give birth to live young)

5. **Lizards**

6. Turtles and tortoises

7. **Frogs and toads (but some kinds give birth to live young)**

8. Salamanders (the fire salamander and some other kinds give birth to live young)

9. **Insects (most insects lay eggs but a few give birth to live young)**

10. Spiders

11. **Crustaceans (some crayfish give birth to live young)**

12. Centipedes and millipedes

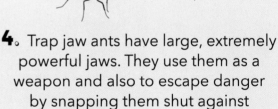

6 Interesting Ants

1. **Bullet ants, which live in rain forests, are said to have the most painful sting in the world—the pain is like being shot with a bullet.**

2. Army ants are expert builders and can make a living bridge by clasping onto each other's limbs as they stretch across a chasm.

3. **Leaf-cutter ants cut and carry bits of leaves back to their nest—not to eat, but to farm. The rotting leaves decompose and produce fungus that the ant colony eats.**

4. Trap jaw ants have large, extremely powerful jaws. They use them as a weapon and also to escape danger by snapping them shut against the ground, which propels the ant up and away from danger.

5. **Dracula ants from Madagascar survive by sucking the blood of their own larvae (without killing them!).**

6. The carpenter ant makes the ultimate sacrifice to protect the colony. When under attack it explodes, killing itself but coating the enemy in toxic chemicals.

9 LAZY Animals

If you're ever accused of being lazy, simply point to these animals, which really are total lazers. The numbers in brackets are the average number of hours each animal sleeps per day.

1. **Little brown bat (20)**
2. North American possum (18)
3. **Burmese python (18)**
4. Owl monkey (17)
5. **Night monkey (17)**
6. Three-toed sloth (15)
7. **Koala (14)**
8. American badger (14)
9. **Elegant fat-tailed mouse possum (14)**

7 KINDS of Deer

1. **Moose, the largest of all deer, with antlers that can measure over 6 feet (1.8 m) from end to end.**
2. Pudú, the smallest deer on earth at 16 inches (40 cm) high at the shoulder, with antlers up to 2.8 inches (7 cm) long.
3. **Reindeer**   4. Sambar deer
5. **Muntjac**   6. Red deer
7. **Barasingha deer**

5 BUSY ANIMALS

1. **Bees are famously busy. To produce just 0.09 oz (2.5 ml) of honey, a honeybee has to work 10 hours a day for 6 days. Meanwhile the queen honeybee is busy laying more than a thousand eggs a day.**

2. Shrews have a fast metabolism and have to be on the lookout for food at all times—they barely have time for a nap.

3. **All kinds of ants work very long hours gathering food, defending the colony, cleaning up, and looking after babies. Some kinds can lift loads up to 50 times their size.**

4. Arctic terns are almost always on the move, migrating to and from Antarctica, the longest migration distance of all birds. Each way takes at least 90 days with hardly any breaks. In a lifetime, a single Arctic tern flies about 1.5 million miles (2.4 million km).

5. **Beavers are constantly beavering away, building dams across rivers and streams, and homes for themselves out of branches and mud.**

7 Facts About Toucans

. . . .

1. There are 40 different kinds of toucan, ranging in size from 7 inches (18 cm) to over 24 inches (60 cm) tall. They all live in the tropical forests of South America.

2. Toucans all have very large bills, but the toco toucan's is the largest—its beak is one-third of its body length.

3. Toucan beaks may be big but they're not heavy. They're made of keratin (the same stuff that hair and nails are made from), with lots of air pockets to make them very light.

4. The birds use their outsized beaks to pluck and peel fruit, their main source of food.

5. Toucans also have a long, flat tongue, which they use to catch insects, frogs, and reptiles.

6. Toucans can control their body temperature by adjusting blood flow to their beaks. When they sleep, they tuck their beak under their feathers to keep it warm.

7. Although they spend a lot of time in trees, they are not great at flying. Toucans mainly travel between trees by hopping.

19 TYPES of RODENT

Rodents are the largest group of mammals, and there are more than 2,000 different kinds. Here are just a few:

1. Mice **2.** Rats **3.** Hamsters

4. Guinea pigs **5.** Gerbils **6.** Chinchillas

7. Beavers **8.** Muskrats **9.** Porcupines

10. Woodchucks **11.** Chipmunks **12.** Squirrels

13. Prairie dogs **14.** Marmots **15.** Voles

16. Lemmings **17.** Coypus **18.** Agoutis

19. Capybaras

5 GREAT Apes

1. **Humans**
2. Gorillas
3. **Orangutans**
4. Chimpanzees
5. **Bonobos**

6 Unusual Bird Beaks

1. **The great white pelican has a huge beak with a stretchy pouch underneath that folds away when not in use. The pouch is used to scoop up large catches of fish like a fishing net.**

2. The rhinoceros hornbill has an enormous hollow structure called a casque on top of its already massive beak. The casque, which is bright red and yellow, curves upwards like a rhino's horn.

3. **The sword-billed hummingbird has a beak longer than the rest of its body. It uses it to get at the nectar in flowers with long petals.**

4. Avocets are wading birds with long, thin beaks that curve upward. They use their beaks to stir up small creatures in shallow water, then snap up their prey.

5. **Spoonbills use their spoon-shaped beaks to stir up shallow water too.**

6. The long-billed curlew is another wading bird with an impressive beak—it's long, thin, and curved, and can measure 8 inches (20 cm) or more.

5

ANIMALS that LIGHT UP

· · · · · · · · · · · · · · · · · · ·

All these animals are bioluminescent—they produce light from a chemical reaction inside their bodies.

1. Fireflies are beetles that live in temperate and tropical climates. They light up at dusk to attract mates or prey.

2. The clusterwink snail is a sea snail that lives off the coasts of Australia. It flashes on and off when it feels threatened.

3. The firefly squid is found in the depths of the western Pacific Ocean. Its mantle, head, arms, and tentacles are dotted with tiny, light-producing organs that flash to lure in small fish, which the squid feeds on.

4. Lanternfish, found in the Red Sea, have light-producing organs along their bodies and another light organ that acts like a headlight.

5. The mauve stinger jellyfish is a glowing sea creature found in deeper waters of the Atlantic.

5

Facts ABOUT Fireflies

1. There are around 2,000 different species of firefly, but not all of them glow.

2. The species that do light up all have their own flashing pattern. A few kinds shake their abdomens from side to side so that they seem to twinkle.

3. When they're threatened, some fireflies shed drops of blood containing bitter-tasting chemicals that are poisonous to birds and lizards.

4. Firefly light can be yellow, green, or orange.

5. Firefly larvae's favourite food is snails. Adult fireflies usually eat pollen and nectar, and some kinds don't eat at all.

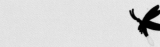

7 ENORMOUS Elephant Facts

1. Elephants are the biggest land animal in the world. Male African elephants can measure 10 feet (3 m) tall and weigh up to 7.5 tons.

2. An elephant's trunk is a joined-up nose and upper lip. Elephants use them to smell things, pick things up, suck up water, and touch one another. Trunks have 40,000 muscles!

3. African elephants spend up to 18 hours a day eating grass and other plants.

4. All that food means that each elephant produces about a 2,200 pounds of poop a week.

5. Asian elephants are smaller and have smaller ears than their African cousins, and an Asian elephant's ears are shaped like a map of India.

6. A hundred years ago, there were more than 3 million African elephants in the wild, but today there are only about 415,000.

7. There are even fewer wild Asian elephants—about 40,000.

11 TYPES of LEMUR

Lemurs are related to monkeys and apes and are found only on the African island of Madagascar. Sadly, they are the most endangered primates in the world, mainly because of the destruction of their tropical forest habitat. Altogether there are 101 different species, from the tiny 1-ounce (30-gram) Madame Berthe's mouse lemur, to the chunky indri lemur that weighs 21 pounds (9.5 kg). Here are a few of them:

1. **Hairy-eared dwarf lemur**
2. Madame Berthe's mouse lemur
3. **Coquerel's giant mouse lemur**
4. Pale fork-marked lemur
5. **White-fronted brown lemur**
6. Blue-eyed black lemur
7. **Mongoose lemur**
8. Golden bamboo lemur
9. **Ring-tailed lemur**
10. Red ruffed lemur
11. **Indri lemur**

4 Animals THAT Can Walk on Water

1. **Water striders are insects that can walk on the water's surface without breaking the surface tension.**
2. Fishing spiders have water-repellent hairs that keep them afloat.

3. **Pygmy geckos are light enough to rest on the water's surface, and have water-repellent skin, too.**
4. Basilisk lizards can run on water on their hind legs for about 15 feet (4.5 m).

Nocturnal Animals

All of these animals come out when the sun goes down:

1. Moths (most kinds, but there are some daytime moths)

2. Owls (some kinds hunt at dawn and dusk, some during the night, and a few kinds of owl hunt during the day)

3. Bats (most kinds, but there are a few that come out during the day)

4. Gray wolf

5. **Raccoon**

6. Aye-aye (a monkey-like animal from Madagascar)

7. Slow loris (a monkey-like animal from Southeast Asia)

8. Red panda

9. Sugar glider (a possum from Australia and Indonesia)

10. Panamanian night monkey (the only nocturnal monkey)

11. Tasmanian devil (a marsupial animal that lives only in Tasmania)

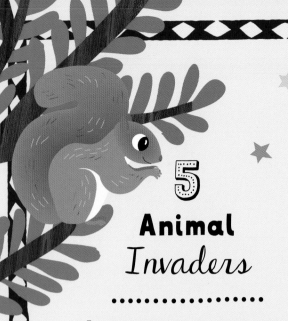

5
Animal Invaders

....

1. Gray squirrels are native to eastern North America but were introduced to Britain in the 1870s. They're now widespread in the UK, where they threaten the survival of the native red squirrel.

2. The Cajun crayfish from the United States was introduced to Africa, where it has no natural predators and preys on fish, crabs, and shellfish.

3. Rabbits were introduced to Australia when Europeans settled there at the end of the 18th century. Within a few decades they had spread throughout most of Australia, devastating plants and animals.

4. Mink were imported to the UK from America and farmed for their fur in the 1950s. Escaped mink have spread throughout the UK, and eat lots of different native wildlife, especially water voles.

5. European starlings were introduced to North America with a devastating impact on American bird species.

33
National ANIMALS

Here are just some of the many creatures claimed by countries around the world as their national animal. As you can see, lions are especially popular.

1. AFRICAN LION
—Ethiopia, England, Gambia, Kenya, Libya, Luxembourg, Morocco, Norway, Sierra Leone, Sri Lanka

2. ANDEAN CONDOR—Colombia

3. ARABIAN CAMEL—Eritrea

4. BAIRD'S TAPIR—Belize

5. BALD EAGLE AND AMERICAN BISON
—United States of America

6. BENGAL TIGER—Bangladesh

7. BLACK PANTHER—Gabon

8. BROWN BEAR—Finland

9. BULL—Spain

10. COW—Nepal

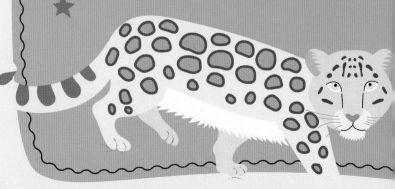

11. **DOLPHIN**—Greece

12. **FALLOW DEER**
—Antigua and Barbuda

13. **FENNEC FOX**—Algeria

14. **GALLIC ROOSTER**—France

15. **GIANT PANDA AND
RED-CROWNED CRANE**—China

16. **EURASIAN BROWN BEAR**—Russia

17. **GIRAFFE**—Tanzania

18. **GOLDEN EAGLE**—Mexico

19. **HARPY EAGLE**—Panama

20. **ASIAN ELEPHANT**—Thailand

21. **KIWI**—New Zealand

22. **KOMODO DRAGON**—Indonesia

23. **LYNX**—Romania

24. **LEOPARD**—Rwanda

25. **MALAYAN TIGER**—Malaysia

26. **NORTH AMERICAN BEAVER**
—Canada

27. **OKAPI**—Democratic Republic
of the Congo

28. **PINE MARTEN**—Croatia

29. **RED KANGAROO AND EMU**
—Australia

30. **RED KITE**—Wales

31. **SNOW LEOPARD**—Afghanistan

32. **VICUÑA**—Peru

33. **WHITE STORK**—Lithuania

7 Types of Octopus

Octopuses are found in seas all over the world, especially in warmer waters. These amazing animals are able to change color in order to blend in with their surroundings or to communicate with other octopuses.

1. **Blue-ringed octopus, which looks pretty but is extremely dangerous.**

2. Mimic octopus, which can mimic 15 different kinds of sea creature.

3. **North Pacific giant octopus, the largest kind in the world, measuring up to 15 feet (4.5 m) long.**

4. Seven-arm octopus—most octopuses have eight arms, but the eighth arm on this octopus has evolved into a small sac underneath the animal's eyes.

5. **Coconut octopus, which uses coconut shells and large seashells to shelter in.**

6. Dumbo octopus, which has fins that look a bit like Dumbo the Disney elephant's ears.

7. **Caribbean reef octopus, which has the best camouflage skills of any octopus.**

7 Animals that Can Live for MORE THAN 100 YEARS

1. Red sea urchins can live for more than 200 years.

2. Koi carp usually live for 25-30 years, but some live much longer. A famous koi named Hanako died in 1977—from the growth rings on her scales, she was found to have been 226 years old.

3. Longfin eels often reach around 60 years old, but the oldest ever recorded was 106.

4. The Galapagos tortoise, the largest kind alive today, can live to be well over 100.

5. Bowhead whales have an average lifespan of 200 years.

6. Greenland sharks grow very slowly (about 0.5 inches/1 cm a year), reach maturity when they're about 100, and often live more than 200 years.

7. Ocean quahogs are a type of clam that can live for hundreds of years. The highest reported age is 507—a clam named Ming that died in 2006 and would have been alive during the Ming Chinese Dynasty.

11 Spotted Animals

1. Giraffe
2. Cheetah
3. Leopard
4. Dalmatian dog
5. Fallow deer
6. Appaloosa horse
7. Ladybird spider
8. Spotted moray eel
9. Ladybug
10. Blue buckeye butterfly
11. Yellow-spotted wolf snake

RECORD-BREAKING *Cats*
3

1. **Didga the cat holds the world record for number of tricks performed by a cat in one minute. She managed 24, which included rolling over and jumping over a bar while riding a skateboard.**

2. The longest cat's whiskers belong to Missie the Maine coon cat—her longest whisker measured 7.5 inches (19 cm).

3. **Waffle the Warrior Cat made the longest jump ever recorded by a cat—84 inches (213.36 cm).**

RECORD-BREAKING
DOGS
3

1. **The world record for the longest human tunnel travelled through by a dog on a skateboard is held by Otto the bulldog.**

2. Augie the golden retriever holds the world record for the highest number of tennis balls held in the mouth by a dog—five.

3. **A bloodhound called Tigger has the longest recorded ears on a dog—his right ear measured 13.74 inches (34.9 cm), and the left 13.46 inches (34.2 cm).**

13 TYPES of PONY

1. **Shetland pony**
2. Exmoor pony
3. **Dartmoor pony**
4. Connemara
5. **Eriskay**
6. Gotland pony
7. **Dales pony**
8. Chincoteague pony
9. **Faroe pony**
10. Anadolu pony
11. **British spotted pony**
12. Dulmen pony
13. **New Forest pony**

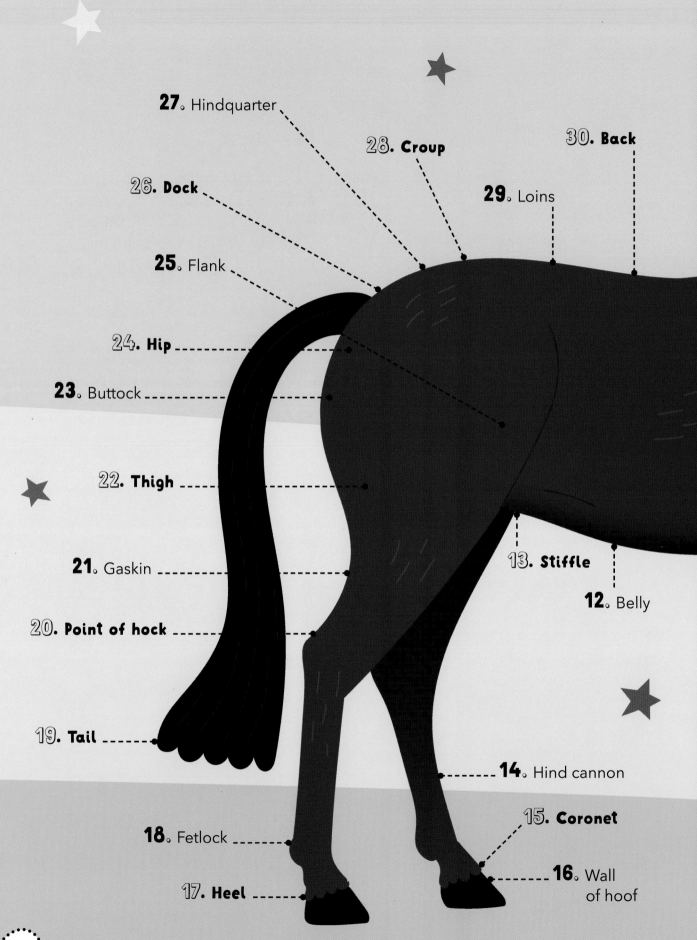

27. Hindquarter

28. Croup

30. Back

26. Dock

29. Loins

25. Flank

24. Hip

23. Buttock

22. Thigh

13. Stiffle

21. Gaskin

12. Belly

20. Point of hock

19. Tail

14. Hind cannon

15. Coronet

18. Fetlock

16. Wall
of hoof

17. Heel

35. Poll

34. Crest

33. Mane

32. Neck

31. Withers

1. Forelock

2. Facial crest

3. Muzzle

5. Throat

4. Chin groove

6. Jugular groove

7. Shoulder

8. Forearm

9. Knee

10. Forecannon

11. Pastern

35
PARTS of a
HORSE

12 STRIPED Animals

1. **Zebra**
2. Tiger
3. **Okapi**
4. Zebra cichlid (aka convict fish)
5. **Kudu (an antelope)**
6. Three-striped poison frog
7. **Zebra-striped swallowtail butterfly**
8. Chipmunk
9. **Six-lined racerunner (a lizard)**
10. Striped pajama squid
11. **Bongo (an antelope)**
12. Numbat (an Australian marsupial)

30 Popular Breeds of Dog

. . . .

1. **Australian shepherd** 2. Basset hound
3. **Beagle** 4. Border collie 5. **Boxer** 6. Bulldog
7. **Cocker spaniel** 8. Chihuahua 9. **Dachshund**
10. Doberman pinscher 11. **French bulldog**
12. German shepherd 13. **Golden retriever**
14. Great Dane 15. **Labrador retriever**
16. Maltese 17. **Newfoundland**
18. Pembroke Welsh corgi 19. **Pomeranian**
20. Poodle 21. **Pug** 22. Rottweiler
23. **Scottish terrier** 24. Shih tzu
25. **Siberian husky** 26. Springer spaniel
27. **Vizsla** 28. Weimaraner
29. **West Highland terrier**
30. Yorkshire terrier

5 Fishy Facts

1. **Fish have been around for more than 500 million years.**

2. There are around 32,000 kinds of fish alive today, which is more than all mammal, bird, reptile, and amphibian species put together.

3. **Fish get their oxygen from water using their gills.**

4. Some fish can survive out of water—lungfish can survive buried in the mud, extracting oxygen from the air.

5. **Down in the deep, dark oceans, more than a thousand kinds of fish glow in the dark.**

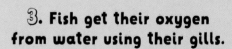

6 UNPLEASANT CURES
Involving *Animals*

Read this list and then take a moment
to be thankful for modern medicine.

**1. In Ancient Egypt, a cure for toothache
was to apply a dead mouse to the tooth.**

**2. A medieval cure for the Black Death was
to strap a live chicken next to the sores.**

**3. An Ancient Egyptian cure for baldness was to mix
together fat from a hippo, a crocodile, a cat, a snake,
and an ibex, and rub the mixture over the bald head.**

**4. A Saxon cure for stomachache was to catch
a beetle and throw it over your shoulder.**

**5. In Ancient Rome, a cure for toothache was to
catch a frog at full moon, spit in its mouth, then
tell it to go away and take the toothache with it.**

**6. In Ancient Britain, a cure for baldness was to
bury a jar of dead mice beside a fire, then dig it up a
year later and rub what's left of the mice onto the head.**

4 RECORD-BREAKING FISH

**1. The world's biggest fish is
the whale shark, over 31 feet
(9.5 m) long and 20 tons in weight.**

**2. The world's smallest fish only has a
Latin name—*Paedocypris progenetica*.
It measures less than 0.3 inches (8 mm).**

**3. The black marlin is thought
to be the world's fastest fish,
belting along at 80 miles per
hour (129 km/h).**

**4. Greenland sharks are
the fish with the longest
lifespan—they can live
for more than
200 years.**

10 GREEN ANIMALS

1. **Green sweat bee**
2. Australian green tree frog
3. **Green sea slug**
4. Three-toed sloth (not actually green, but looks green because green algae grows on its fur)
5. **Roscoff worm (or mint sauce worm)**
6. Green anaconda
7. **Green orbweaver spider**
8. Kakapo (a flightless parrot)
9. **Lunar moth**
10. Manus green tree snail (with an emerald-green shell)

6 ENORMOUS
Predators

1. **Orca—one of the world's most powerful marine predators. Up to 33 feet (10 m) long and 6.6 tons in weight.**

2. Polar bear—the world's largest land carnivore. Males can weigh up to 1,765 pounds (800 kg).

3. **Tiger—the world's largest cat. Can weigh up to 800 pounds (360 kg).**

4. Lion—the world's second-largest cat. Can weigh up to 500 pounds (225 kg).

5. **Saltwater crocodile—the biggest reptile in the world. Can weigh up to 1 ton.**

6. Great white shark—up to 5,000 pounds (2,250 kg) in weight with more than 300 razor-sharp teeth.

6 Animal DEFENSES

Avoiding being eaten is a high priority for many animals, and they've developed all sorts of ways of doing it.

1. PLAYING DEAD
And to be really convincing, smelling terrible at the same time. Opossums and southern hognose snakes are two of the animals that do this.

2. WARNING CALLS
Animals who live in groups keep a lookout and sound the alarm when danger approaches to warn the others. Meerkats do this, and have different calls depending on how severe the threat is.

3. SAFETY IN NUMBERS
Living in big groups means an animal is far more likely to survive an attack by predators—and a group poses a bigger threat to predators.

4. CAMOUFLAGE
This allows animals to blend in with their surroundings to mask their identity. Fish such as flounders look very similar to their speckled seafloor home.

5. ARMOR AND WEAPONS
Some animals have built-in defenses. Tortoises and armadillos have hard shells, and porcupines have sharp quills.

6. CREATING A STINK
Predators tend to steer clear of foul-smelling animals. Skunks can spray a terrible-smelling liquid as far as 10 feet (3 m).

5 Animals with HUGE Eyes

1. TARSIER MONKEYS
Super-cute monkeys from southeast Asia with little tufts on the ends of their hairless tails. Their huge eyes help them to see in the dark.

2. JAVAN SLOW LORIS
Lorises' big, round eyes give them excellent night vision. The reflection of their eyes can be visible from at least 1,000 feet (300 m) away.

3. THE RUFOUS NET-CASTING SPIDER
These spindly spiders have eight eyes, but two of them are absolutely huge.

4. COLOSSAL SQUID
The largest eyes on any animal in the world (even including blue whales), and also the largest animal without a backbone. The eyes are about 10.6 inches (27 cm) wide.

5. OSTRICH
These fast-running, flightless African birds have eyes that are bigger than their brains. Mind you, they are not famous for their IQ.

4
Animals with MORE THAN ONE HEART

1. **Earthworms have five pairs of heartlike structures known as arches.**

2. Octopuses have three hearts.

3. **Squids have three hearts too.**

4. Hagfish have four hearts.

7 DEEP-SEA CREATURES

All sorts of strange creatures are lurking in the deep, dark depths.

1. **Spider crabs are the largest crustaceans in the world—males grow to about 3 feet (1 m) long, with a 13-foot (4-m) leg span. They live at depths of up to 1,300 feet (400 m), in cold seas off the coast of Japan.**

2. Giant isopods look like creepy sea woodlice. They can grow up to 12 inches (30 cm) long and live on the seabed at depths of 1,640 feet (500 m) or more.

3. **Goblin sharks live at depths of more than 4,265 feet (1,300 m). They can completely unhinge their jaws when feeding.**

4. **Atlantic wolffish are toothy fish that live at depths of 5,250 feet (1,600 m).**

5. Giant tube worms live at the edge of hydrothermal vents, which spew chemicals and super-hot water, at depths of 7,875 feet (2,400) m or more.

6. **Vampire squid are named for their dark, webbed arms, which they can draw over themselves like a cloak. They live at depths of around 10,000 feet (3,000 m).**

7. Fangtooth fish are especially ugly and the deepest-living fish ever discovered. They have been found swimming at depths of 16,400 feet (5,000 m).

9 RED Animals

1. **Ladybug**
2. Scarlet ibis
3. **Red starfish**
4. Scarlet lily beetle
5. **Sinaloan milksnake**
6. Strawberry poison frog
7. **Velvet ant**
8. Eurasian red squirrel
9. **East Pacific red octopus**

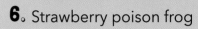

7 PREHISTORIC SEA CREATURES

1. ELASMOSAURUS
A long-necked marine reptile that lived 85–65 million years ago. It used its long neck to sneak up on shoals of fish.

2. MEGALODON
The largest shark (and the largest fish) that ever lived, as far as we know. It ruled the seas until 2.6 million years ago, and the largest specimens could reach more than 49 feet (15 m) long.

3. DAKOSAURUS
A fearsome predator with a powerful bite and huge teeth. It lived 157–137 million years ago.

4. BASILOSAURUS
A primitive whale that was the largest known marine mammal when it was alive, 55.8 million to 33.9 million years ago.

5. SHASTASAURUS
Marine reptiles that were probably filter feeders, slurping up little cephalopods. It lived 235–205 million years ago.

6. PROTOSTEGA GIGAS
An enormous turtle that fed on jellyfish, shellfish, and floating carcasses around 85 million years ago.

7. DUNKLEOSTEUS
An armor-plated fish with razor-sharp, snapping jaws that lived until 358 million years ago.

6 RIVERBANK
Animals

1. Water voles live in burrows in the riverbank. They're sometimes called water rats, but they're different animals.

2. European otters feed on fish, birds, frogs, and shellfish.

3. Eurasian beavers are river engineers, damming rivers and digging canal systems.

4. Water shrews hunt for insects and their larvae and can swim underwater.

5. Kingfishers hunt from the banks of slow-moving rivers.

6. Dragonflies are super fast, catching other insects as they fly.

6 RIVER ANIMALS

1. Pike—can grow to 3 feet (1 m) long. They prey on fish, frogs, small mammals, and ducklings.

2. Brown trout—also predatory fish, with rows of sharp teeth.

3. Three-spined sticklebacks—small but aggressive predators that eat tadpoles, smaller fish, and insects.

4. Water boatmen—have long back legs that they use to swim along the surface of the water.

5. Dragonfly nymphs—the larvae of dragonfly and fierce underwater predators.

6. Eels—born in the Sargasso sea, can live to be 100 years old.

6 ANIMAL Vampires

All of these creatures have an appetite for blood.

1. Vampire bats make a small cut in a large mammal, then lap up the blood.

2. Lampreys are fish that feed on the blood of other fish by latching onto them with hooklike teeth.

3. Ticks are tiny but can drink up to 600 times their own body weight in blood.

4. Mosquitos are responsible for more human deaths than any other animal because some types can pass on a range of diseases, including deadly malaria.

5. Leeches live in rivers and streams. They attach themselves to a passing animal and drink until they're full, then drop off.

6. Vampire moths suck blood from large animals such as buffalo.

7 Facts ABOUT GIANT PANDAS

1. Pandas live in thick bamboo forests, high up in the mountains of central China.

2. They have very big appetites, and spend up to 12 hours a day eating to get through a whopping 26.5 pounds (12 kg) of bamboo in a day.

3. Pandas are omnivores and will occasionally eat small animals and fish, but bamboo makes up 99 percent of their diet.

4. Unlike most other bears, pandas don't hibernate. Instead, they move down the mountain to warmer areas in the winter.

5. Giant pandas are solitary, but they have a highly developed sense of smell that males use to avoid one another, and to find females for mating in the spring.

6. A newborn panda has a white coat and is almost completely helpless. It depends on its mother for warmth, food, and going to the bathroom (a baby panda's mother has to stimulate it to make it poop). It starts to walk when it's about 75 days old.

7. Fossils found in Myanmar and Vietnam show that the giant panda once roamed throughout eastern Asia.

3 ANIMAL *World* RECORDS

1. **The longest-living land animals are giant tortoises. The oldest alive today is Jonathan, who is over 187 years old.**

2. Ostriches lay the world's biggest eggs–the largest on record weighed 5.69 pounds (2.58 kg).

3. **The tallest animal on Earth is the giraffe, which stands up to 20 feet (6 m) tall.**

4 ANIMALS *that are* Surprisingly Good Swimmers

1. **Unlike most cats, tigers are excellent swimmers thanks to their strong bodies and webbed paws.**

2. Although sloths move slowly and awkwardly across land, they can move well through water using their long arms to propel themselves along.

3. **Elephants are the world's largest land mammal, but they're also good swimmers if they can find somewhere deep enough.**

4. Adult moose can run up to 14 miles per hour (22 km/h), and they're excellent swimmers too.

6 *Cute* Koala FACTS

1. **Koalas get their name from an Aboriginal term meaning "no drink" –koalas get almost all of their moisture from eucalyptus leaves and rarely drink water.**

2. They spend up to 18 hours a day asleep in the branches of eucalyptus trees.

3. **Koalas have a big appetite and can eat up to 2 pounds (1 kg) of eucalyptus leaves in a day.**

4. Although people call them "koala bears," they're actually a marsupial, a group of mammals that have pouches in which newborns develop.

5. **A baby koala is called a joey and spends the first year of its life with its mother. It spends the first six months in its mother's pouch, and then the next six months riding on her back, only using the pouch to feed and sleep.**

6. A newborn koala is the size of a broad bean.

16 Types
of SHARK

There are more than 400 types of shark in the world, most of them completely harmless to people. Here is a small selection.

1. **Whale shark**
2. Basking shark
3. **Bull shark**
4. Tiger shark
5. **Great white shark**
6. Blue shark
7. **Hammerhead shark**
8. Nurse shark
9. **Blacktip reef shark**
10. Lemon shark
11. **Megamouth shark**
12. Leopard shark
13. **Pajama shark**
14. Cookiecutter shark
15. **Crocodile shark**
16. Longfin mako shark

12 AMAZING
Things ABOUT BATS

1. **There are over a thousand different species of bats, which account for around 20 percent of all mammal species.**

2. Bats use echolocation—they make noises and build up a picture of what's around them as the sound bounces back.

3. **Bats are the only mammals able to fly, and some kinds can fly at speeds up to 59 miles per hour (95 km/h).**

4. Bats do not make nests, but roost in buildings, caves, or hollow trees.

5. **The world's largest bat, the flying fox, has a wingspan of up to 5 feet (1.5 m).**

6. The world's smallest bat is the Kitti's hog-nosed bat, which weighs around 0.1 oz (2 g). Its body is about the size of a large bumblebee.

7. **Three of the bat species are vampire bats, which drink blood as their source of food.**

7 Myths ABOUT Animals that Aren't TRUE

1. Bats are blind. No, they're not! Many smaller kinds of bats use echolocation as their main way of "seeing" the world, but they can see as well. Fruit bats have better eyesight than humans.

2. Goldfish can't remember anything for longer than a few seconds. Yes, they can! In fact, goldfish have quite good memories and can learn things.

3. Bulls charge when they see the color red. In fact, bulls are color blind.

4. Elephant trunks are like straws. Trunks are used to breathe, smell, and gather food, but they aren't used as straws. Elephants can use them to suck up and squirt water into their mouths though.

5. Ostriches bury their heads in the sand. Ostriches sometimes check on their eggs buried in a hole in the ground, so maybe that's where this saying comes from.

6. Owls can do a 360-degree head spin. That would be impossible (think about it), but owls can manage a swivel of up to 270 degrees, which is still pretty impressive.

7. All bees only sting once and then they die. This is true of honeybees but not other kinds.

8. In one year, a colony of 100 vampire bats can drain the blood of 25 cows.

9. The world needs bats! Some plants depend either partly or wholly on bats to pollinate their flowers or spread their seeds, and some bats also help control pests by eating insects.

10. Bats can eat up to 1,200 mosquitos an hour.

11. Bat poop can be used to make gunpowder. Known as guano, bat droppings are high in potassium nitrate and are often used in fertilizer, as well as olden-days gunpowder.

12. Nearly all the bat species hang upside down, but there are six species that don't. These bats have suctioning pads on their limbs that let them stick to leaves or other surfaces.

13 Types
of DUCK

1. **Harlequin duck**
2. Spectacled eider
3. **White-faced whistling duck**
4. Wood duck
5. **Hooded merganser**
6. Shelduck
7. **Mallard**
8. Baikal teal
9. **Pink-eared duck**
10. Muscovy duck
11. **Freckled duck**
12. Surf scooter duck
13. **White-headed duck**

6 Flying Insect Facts

1. Insects first began to fly around 300 million years ago.

2. **Most insects have two pairs of wings —grasshoppers, bees, wasps, dragonflies, butterflies, and moths all have two pairs —but true flies, including house flies and mosquitos, have only one pair.**

3. The fastest wingbeat of any flying insect belongs to the midge, whose wings beat 62,760 times per minute.

4. **The smallest known flying insect is a type of fairyfly that is only 0.005 inches (0.139 mm) long.**

5. The biggest flying insect is a type of dobsonfly. It has a wingspan of 8.3 inches (21 cm) and a body up to 4 inches (10.5) cm long.

6. **The biggest insect wingspan is 11 inches (28 cm) and belongs to the beautiful Queen Alexandra's birdwing butterfly.**

10 Facts ABOUT DUCKS, GEESE, and Swans

1. **These water birds have waterproof feathers and webbed feet that they use as flippers to push them through the water.**

2. Ducks, geese, and swans are found all across the world, except for Antarctica.

3. **Most live in freshwater wetlands, estuaries, and inshore coastal waters, but there are a few marine species.**

4. Most ducks, geese, and swans migrate huge distances every year between their summer breeding grounds and the regions where they spend the winter.

5. **The bar-headed goose flies over the Himalayan mountains during its migration and reaches a height of 21,119 feet (6,437 m), the highest flight of any known bird.**

6. Ducks and geese use thousands of different muscles in their skin to control their feathers. This helps them to regulate body heat, dive underwater, and display emotions.

7. **The fastest duck ever recorded, a red-breasted merganser, was clocked at 100 miles per hour (160 km/h).**

8. To be safe from predators, barnacle geese nest on cliffs up to 148 feet (45 m) high along the Greenland coast. When the baby geese hatch they jump off the cliff and fall to the ground or sea below, cushioned by the down feathers on their bodies.

9. **Most ducks, geese, and swans are omnivores and eat plants and insects, and some breeds eat small amphibians.**

10. Geese and swans mate for life, but ducks have a new mate every season.

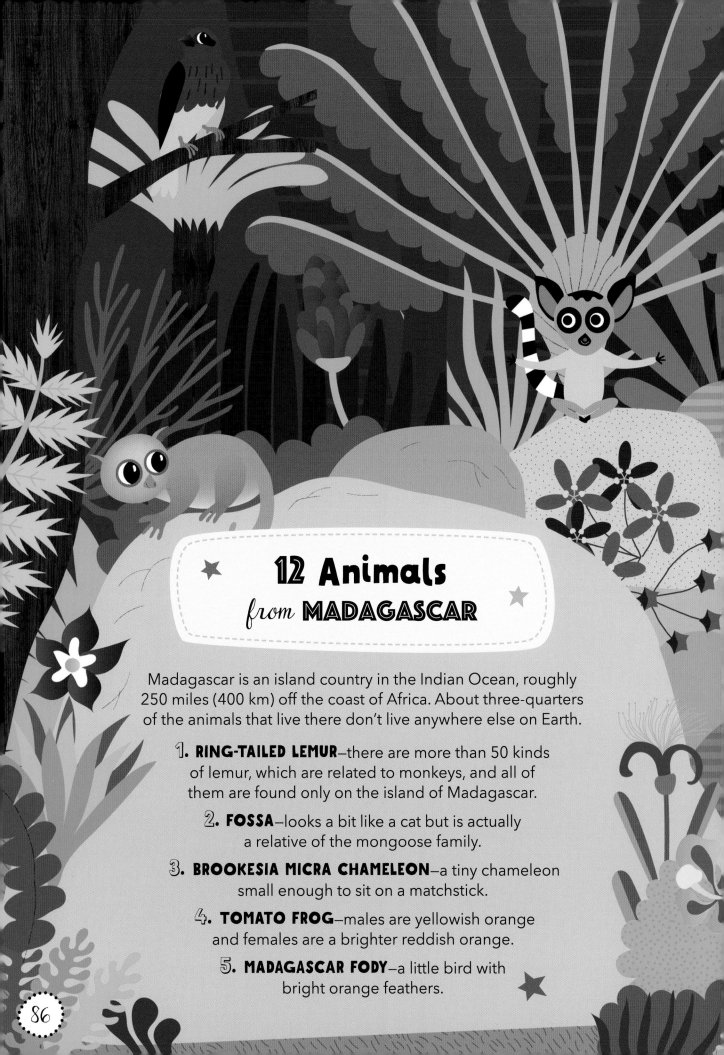

12 Animals
from MADAGASCAR

Madagascar is an island country in the Indian Ocean, roughly 250 miles (400 km) off the coast of Africa. About three-quarters of the animals that live there don't live anywhere else on Earth.

1. **RING-TAILED LEMUR**—there are more than 50 kinds of lemur, which are related to monkeys, and all of them are found only on the island of Madagascar.

2. **FOSSA**—looks a bit like a cat but is actually a relative of the mongoose family.

3. **BROOKESIA MICRA CHAMELEON**—a tiny chameleon small enough to sit on a matchstick.

4. **TOMATO FROG**—males are yellowish orange and females are a brighter reddish orange.

5. **MADAGASCAR FODY**—a little bird with bright orange feathers.

6. AYE-AYE—monkey relative with big ears, ratty teeth, and a strange, long finger adapted for catching its insect prey.

7. MADAGASCAR LONG-EARED OWL—a medium-sized owl with long ear-tufts.

8. LOWLAND STREAKED TENREC—a small mammal with spikes like a hedgehog's.

9. MADAGASCAN MOON MOTH—a green-and-yellow moth.

10. GIRAFFE WEEVIL—a little red insect with a ridiculously long neck.

11. MADAGASCAR SPEAR-NOSED SNAKE—a snake with a very pointy nose.

12. BLUE COUA—a beautiful violet-blue bird.

8 Meerkat Facts

1. Meerkats are a type of mongoose native to the deserts and grasslands of southern Africa, including South Africa, Botswana, Zimbabwe, and Mozambique.

2. They live in big groups of up to 50, often made up of several families.

3. A meerkat weighs about the same as a squirrel (2.2 pounds or 1 kg).

4. Meerkats live in underground burrows, which keeps them cool from the strong African sun and protects them from predators. One burrow can have as many as 15 entrance and exit holes.

5. Meerkats take turns doing shifts of foraging for food, babysitting pups, and watching out for predators such as eagles, hawks, and jackals.

6. Meerkats on lookout perch on their back legs and let out a high-pitched noise to alert other meerkats if they spot danger.

7. Meerkats use their strong sense of smell to sniff out food, which includes insects, spiders, scorpions, small reptiles, and eggs.

8. Scorpions are a favorite food for meerkats. Adult meerkats have some immunity to their venom, and mother meerkats cut off the scorpions' tails so the pups can enjoy the treat too.

6 EXTINCT ANIMALS

1. AUROCH
A wild ox, up to 6 feet (1.8 m) tall, it is the common ancestor of all domestic cattle breeds. It lived until 1627, and was the world's first recorded extinction.

2. DODO
A flightless bird that lived on Mauritius. The last recorded sighting was in 1662.

3. STELLER'S SEA COW
Up to 30 feet (9 m) in length. It was first described in 1741, and had been hunted to extinction by 1768.

4. GREAT AUK
A flightless seabird that lived on rocky islands off North Atlantic coasts. It has been extinct since 1844.

5. GOLDEN TOAD
Lived in the Costa Rican rain forest before being declared extinct in 1994.

6. TASMANIAN TIGER (AKA THE THYLACINE)
A striped wolflike Australian marsupial. The last one died at Hobart Zoo in 1936.

5 PREHISTORIC Animals that Aren't DINOSAURS

1. WOOLLY MAMMOTH
Most died out by 10,500 years ago, but one isolated group lived on until 4,500 years ago.

2. IRISH ELK
Had the largest antler span of all deer at up to 12 feet (3.65 m). It died out between 11,000 and 8,800 years ago.

3. SMILODON
A type of saber-toothed cat that became extinct about 14,000 years ago.

4. DIRE WOLVES
Huge wolves that lived in America. They went extinct 10,000 years ago when their large prey began to die off.

5. GIANT GROUND SLOTH
From South America, it was up to 20 feet (6 m) tall. It died out about 10,500 years ago.

8
ANIMALS WITH MORE than One Stomach

1. **Cattle** 2. Sheep 3. **Deer**
4. Antelope 5. **Goat** 6. Giraffe
7. **Kangaroo** 8. Sperm whale

9
Yellow Animals

1. **Ghost crab**
2. Canary
3. **Yellow tang (a marine fish)**
4. Clouded sulfur butterfly
5. **Yellow warbler (a bird)**
6. Goldenrod crab spider
7. **Burmese python**
8. Panamanian golden frog
9. **Banana slug**

15 Popular Breeds of Rabbit

1. **Lionhead**
2. Flemish giant
3. **Holland lop**
4. Continental giant
5. **Netherland dwarf**
6. Dutch rabbit
7. **English lop**
8. French lop
9. **Mini rex**
10. Polish rabbit
11. **American rabbit**
12. Beveren rabbit
13. **Californian rabbit**
14. American fuzzy lop
15. **American sable rabbit**

14 Creatures Found *in* *Temperate* Woodland

These animals wouldn't necessarily be found in the same woodland, but they all live in forests that don't have extremes of temperature.

1. Red fox
2. **Badger**
3. Tawny owl
4. **Gray squirrel**
5. Dormouse
6. **Red deer**
7. Woodland vole
8. **Beaver**
9. Hedgehog
10. **Common shrew**
11. Black bear
12. **Moose**
13. Chipmunk
14. **Raccoon**

12 Kinds
of Fox

There are 37 different kinds of fox,
but only 12 of them are "true" foxes.
All of them are absolutely adorable.
Here are the 12 kinds of true fox.

1. **Arctic fox** 2. Bengal fox 3. **Blanford's fox**
4. Cape fox 5. **Corsac fox** 6. Fennec fox
7. **Kit fox** 8. Pal fox 9. **Red fox**
10. Ruppell's fox 11. **Swift fox**
12. Tibetan sand fox

12 MARINE *Molluscs*

1. **Squid**
2. Geoduck (a type of clam)
3. **Octopus**
4. Cuttlefish
5. **Spirula (a bit like a squid)**
6. Nautilus (a shelled mollusc)
7. **Sea butterfly (a type of sea snail)**
8. Nudibranch (also known as sea slugs)
9. **Sea hare (a sea slug with an internal shell)**
10. Limpet
11. **Scallop**
12. Oyster

18 Types *of* SEAL

1. **Leopard seal**
2. Gray seal
3. **Bearded seal**
4. Harbor seal
5. **Spotted seal**
6. Ringed seal
7. **Baikal seal**
8. Harp seal
9. **Ribbon seal**
10. Hooded seal
11. **Weddell seal**
12. Caspian seal
13. **Crabeater seal**
14. Ross seal
15. **Southern elephant seal**
16. Northern elephant seal
17. **Mediterranean monk seal**
18. Hawaiian monk seal

6 Really UGLY ANIMALS

• • • • • • • • • • • • • • • • •

1. Blobfish are deep-water fish. They look like a gelatin with a sad face.

2. Naked mole rats are hairless pink rodents with two sharp, yellowish, prominent front teeth.

3. Star-nosed moles have a kind of wiggling starfish-like protrusion on their noses. They use it to sniff out worms and insects.

4. The aye-aye is related to monkeys and apes and has a single weird, long finger on one of its hands that it uses to coax out insects. It's so ugly that it's seen as an omen of bad luck.

5. Proboscis monkeys have long, floppy noses that look ugly to us, but not to other proboscis monkeys.

6. Fly River turtles are also known as pig-nosed turtles because of their huge, fleshy snouts.

14 Types of Starfish

1. Common starfish

2. Spiny starfish

3. Cushion starfish

4. Bloody Henry starfish

5. Morning sun star

6. Sunflower star

7. Royal starfish

8. Crown-of-thorns starfish

9. Nine-armed sea star

10. Chocolate chip sea star

11. Arctic cookie star

12. Pincushion star

13. Giant spined star

14. Necklace starfish

7 Recently Discovered Animals

1. OLINGUITO
Mammal with large eyes and woolly fur, native to the cloud forests of Colombia and Ecuador, discovered in 2013.

2. SAOLA
Horned mammal found only in the Annamite mountains of Vietnam and Laos, discovered in 2010.

3. TOSANOIDES APHRODITE
Pink-and-yellow reef fish, discovered in 2018 on the islands of St. Paul's Rocks off the coast of Brazil.

4. MINI MUM
Teeny tiny frog discovered in Madagascar in 2019.

5. MILTON'S TITI MONKEY
Discovered in Brazil in 2011.

6. SICHUAN BUSH WARBLER
Small brown bird with a beautiful song found in the mountains of central China in 2015.

7. RUBY SEADRAGON
Discovered off the southern coast of Western Australia in 2015.

5 Animals that LOOK CUTE but Can Kill You

1. **Polar bear**—they look adorable, don't they? But they will happily kill and eat you if they're hungry.

2. **Panda**—do not be fooled by their cuddly looks. They don't eat people, but might attack, and they have very sharp teeth and a powerful bite.

3. **Puffer fish**—potential killers if you eat them. They contain a lethal poison called tetrodotoxin, which is removed by specially trained chefs when puffer fish are prepared as a delicacy.

4. **Blue-ringed octopus**—they have enough venom to kill more than 20 humans with one bite. If the rings are glowing bright blue, you're in trouble.

5. **Poison dart frog**—beautiful but deadly, the golden poison dart frog secretes a lethal toxin.

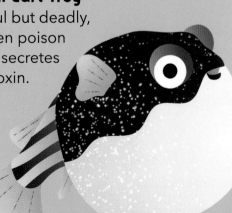

6 Dangerous Scorpions

There are around 1,500 different kinds of scorpion, living all over the world except for Antarctica. Only a few dozen of them are dangerous to humans.

1. The Indian red scorpion, which lives in India, Pakistan, Nepal, and Sri Lanka, is probably the most dangerous of all.

2. The yellow fattail scorpion is found in deserts of North Africa and Southeast Asia, and its sting is potentially deadly to people.

3. The South African fattail scorpion can deliver enough venom to kill an adult.

4. The Brazilian yellow scorpion is the most dangerous scorpion in South America—thousands of people die from its sting every year.

5. The scarily named deathstalker scorpion lives in deserts from North Africa to the Middle East. Its venom is powerful enough to kill children and old or sick people.

6. The bark scorpion is the most venomous scorpion in North America. It can kill if the sting isn't treated quickly enough.

7 PLATYPUS Facts

1. The platypus is only found in freshwater in eastern and southeastern Australia and Tasmania.

2. It's one of the world's strangest animals, with a bill like a duck's and a tail like a beaver's. When it was first sent to England to be examined in the 1800s, scientists thought several animals had been stitched together as a joke.

3. The platypus is one of only two mammals that lays eggs (the other is the echidna).

4. The male platypus is venomous —it has stingers on its back feet.

5. Platypuses are excellent swimmers, using their webbed feet and rudder-like tail. They can close their nostrils, eyes, and ears while they're underwater.

6. They feed on the bottom of rivers and lakes, scooping up shellfish, worms, and other small animals in their bills, along with gravel and mud. Everything is stored in cheek pouches, then eaten when the platypus comes to the surface. The gravel helps it grind up food, because it doesn't have teeth.

7. Platypuses have claws underneath the webbing on their feet, which they use to make burrows on the riverbank.

14 Farmyard ANIMALS

As well as the animals you might expect, some unusual animals are farmed.

1. Chickens 2. **Turkeys** 3. Quails

4. **Guineafowl** 5. Pigs 6. **Goats**

7. Cattle (dairy cows and beef cattle) 8. **Rabbits**

9. Sheep 10. **Alpacas** 11. Llamas

12. **Camels** 13. Ostriches 14. **Emus**

6 Kangaroo *Facts*

1. There are six different kinds of large kangaroos, which all live in Australia and have huge, powerful hind legs for hopping along.

2. The biggest kind is the red kangaroo, which can be 6.5 feet (2 m) tall and weighs 200 pounds (90 kg).

3. Kangaroos live in groups of about 50 individuals.

4. Kangaroos are marsupials—females have a pouch for baby kangaroos, which are called joeys.

5. A joey is only about 1 inch (2.5 cm) long when it's born. It crawls into the safety of its mother's pouch right away.

6. Kangaroos can bound along at more than 34 miles per hour (55 km/h) and cover more than 30 feet (9 m) in one hop.

11 Types *of Jellyfish*

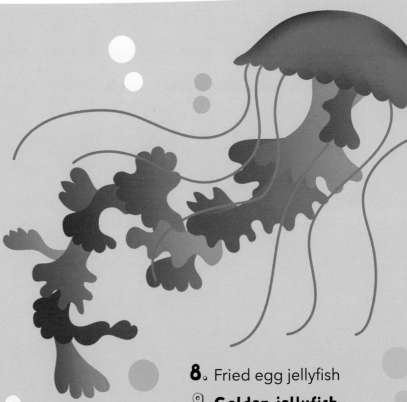

1. Lion's mane jellyfish

2. Upside down jellyfish

3. Moon jellyfish

4. Cauliflower jellyfish

5. White-spotted jellyfish

6. Black sea nettle

7. Flower hat jellyfish

8. Fried egg jellyfish

9. Golden jellyfish

10. Crystal jellyfish

11. Box jellyfish

3 Laughing Animals

1. **Apes—gorillas, chimpanzees, bonobos, and orangutans—all make noises when they're tickled or playing games. Chimps make a noise that sounds more like screeching when they laugh.**

2. Rats make long calls when they're tickled by people and when playing with other rats.

3. **Dolphins make a series of sounds followed by a whistle while play-fighting with other dolphins. Researchers think it is similar to laughter.**

5 Animal Fart FACTS

1. **Herrings gulp air from the surface of the water and use it to fart to communicate with one another.**

2. Termites—small, antlike creatures—fart so much that they make a significant contribution to the world's methane.

3. **Cattle are the worst methane offenders—each individual emits around 220 pounds (100 kg) of methane a year in farts and burps.**

4. Manatees, or sea cows, gulp air to help them float, and fart when they want to dive.

5. **Hippos mark their territory by pooping and farting at the same time, whirling their tails around to spread the poop and the smell across a wide area.**

24 BREEDS OF PIG

1. **Beijing black**
2. Berkshire
3. **British saddleback**
4. Choctaw hog
5. **Duroc**
6. Fengjing
7. **Gascon**
8. Grice
9. **Guinea hog**
10. Hereford
11. **Jeju black**
12. Kunekune
13. **Large black**
14. Latvian white
15. **Livny**
16. Mulefoot
17. **North Caucasian**
18. Norwegian landrace
19. **Oxford sandy and black**
20. Red wattle
21. **Sushan pig**
22. Tamworth
23. **Vietnamese potbelly**
24. Yorkshire blue and white

6 FACTS *about* HONEYBEES

1. Honeybees are insects and live in huge colonies of tens of thousands of bees.

2. They live in nests in the wild, or in hives people build for them so the honey can be harvested.

3. Inside the nest or hive, the bees make a honeycomb made up of hexagonal wax cells. Worker bees use honey to make the wax, which oozes out of small pores in their bodies. The worker bees then chew the wax to make it soft enough to mold into honeycomb.

4. The bees make honey using sugary nectar from flowers. They carry nectar back to the nest, then spit it out into a wax cell, where it turns into honey.

5. There is one large queen bee in each colony. She lays up to 2,000 eggs a day.

6. Honeybees transfer pollen from one plant to another as they gather nectar. Many plants can't reproduce without this help from bees and other insects.

4 GIANT Prehistoric
Creepy Crawlies

Millions of years ago, some creepy crawlies grew to enormous sizes. According to one theory, they got so big because there used to be more oxygen in Earth's atmosphere.

1. Meganeuropsis was a type of griffinfly from about 280 million years ago. One type had a wingspan of more than 24 inches (60 cm) and a body length of more 16 inches (40 cm).

2. Scorpion Pulmonoscorpius lived on land 300 million years ago. It grew to about 27.5 inches (70 cm) long.

3. Jaekelopterus was a scorpionlike sea creature that grew to nearly 8 feet (2.5 m) long. It lived until about 250 million years ago.

4. Arthropleura looked like a millipede but was 20 inches (50 cm) wide and nearly 6.5 feet (2 m) long. It lived until around 299 million years ago.

6 Spotted Hyena Facts

• • • • •

1. There are three different kinds of hyena: the spotted hyena (the most common), the brown, and the striped hyena. They all live in sub-Saharan Africa.

2. A spotted hyena can grow to 6.5 feet (2 m) long and weigh up to 180 pounds (82 kg).

3. Hyenas hunt and kill most of their food, as well as scavenging leftovers of other predators. They eat wildebeest, zebras, baby hippos, and antelope.

4. A hyena's jaw is strong enough to bite through bones.

5. Spotted hyenas live in groups of up to 80. The groups are led by a dominant female.

6. Spotted hyenas are famous for their "laugh"— cackling sounds they use to communicate.

5 PREHISTORIC PTEROSAURS

Pterosaurs swooped around in the sky at the same time dinosaurs stomped around on land. They were the largest animals to fly. They first appeared 215 million years ago and ruled the skies for 150 million years before they became extinct at the same time as the dinosaurs, 65 million years ago. They died out completely—birds and bats aren't related to them.

1. QUETZALCOATLUS
The largest flying animal that's ever lived. It had a wingspan of up to 36 feet (11 m).

2. TUPUXUARA
Had a 20-foot (6-m) wingspan and a crest on its head that measured 4 feet (1.2 m).

3. DSUNGARIPTERUS
Had a hooked beak for prying out shellfish.

4. NEMICOLOPTERUS
The smallest pterosaur that's been discovered so far, with a wingspan of 10 inches (25 cm).

5. EUDIMORPHODON
A fish-eating pterosaur that lived 215 million years ago, one of the very earliest pterosaurs.

3 Talking PARROTS

Some birds, including mynah birds, parrots, budgies, and crows, can mimic human speech. African gray parrots seem to be exceptionally good at it, and these three have become famous.

1. Alex learned around 100 words. He could understand concepts like bigger and smaller, same and different, identify objects by shape and color, and count up to six.

2. Einstein is yet another African gray parrot. He knows 200 words and does impressions of other animals.

3. N'kisi has learned an even more impressive vocabulary of 950 words, and is claimed to be telepathic (able to read the thoughts of others).

6 Facts About Pangolins

1. There are eight species of pangolin, four from Asia and four from Africa.

2. The four Asian pangolins are all listed as "critically endangered." The four African species are "vulnerable."

3. The pangolin's scales are made of keratin, the same stuff that fingernails and hair are made of.

4. Pangolins have long snouts and longer tongues to gobble ants and termites—sometimes they are called "scaly anteaters."

5. Although they look like anteaters and armadillos, pangolins are more closely related to bears.

6. Many thousands of pangolins are hunted and killed every year for their scales, which are used in traditional Chinese medicine, and their meat.

3 MAGICAL Creatures in the HARRY POTTER BOOKS

1. **Acromantula —monster spider**
2. Basilisk—huge snakelike creature
3. **Thestral—meat-eating flying horse**

4 Facts about PRAYING MANTISES

1. **Praying mantises are weird-looking insects, so-called because they hold their front legs up in front of their faces, a bit like praying hands.**

2. They catch and eat other insects, spiders, small lizards, and frogs.

3. **Praying mantises stay very still and strike super-fast when their prey comes close.**

4. Some kinds blend in with their backgrounds to make it easier for them to hide—there's a moss mantis, an orchid mantis, and a dead leaf mantis.

6
Animals
in Space

As well as the animals on this list, cockroaches, jellyfish, snails, newts, mice, scorpions, silkworms, tortoises, and more have all become astronauts.

1. Fruit flies were the first animals to be sent into space, in 1947.

2. Honeybees built a hive during their time in space.

3. A total of 32 monkeys have been sent into space.

4. Chimpanzees named Ham and Enos also became astronauts.

5. Spiders named Arabella and Anita built a messy web in space.

6. Laika the dog was the first animal to orbit the Earth in 1957, and many more dog astronauts followed her.

3 Kinds of ANTEATER

These long-nosed mammals have no teeth but use their ridiculously long tongues to catch and eat up to 30,000 ants per day!

1. The giant anteater has the longest tongue of any animal, which can reach up to 24 inches (60 cm) beyond its mouth! Giant anteaters measure up to 7 feet (2.1 m) from tail to nose.

2. Silky anteaters are nocturnal creatures that live in the treetops of Central and South America. They're so hard to find that a group of scientists searched for two years before they found them to study!

3. Tamandua are anteaters that live throughout South America and grow up to 31.5 inches (80 cm) long. As well as ants and termites, they like to eat bees and honey using their 16-inch (40-cm) tongues.

3 Giant Spiders

1. GOLIATH BIRD-EATING SPIDER
12-inch (30-cm) leg span and 1-inch (2.5-cm) fangs

2. GIANT HUNTSMAN SPIDER
12-inch (30-cm) leg span, but not as hefty as the goliath

3. BRAZILIAN SALMON-PINK BIRD-EATING SPIDER
11-inch (28-cm) leg span

How to Say "BUZZ" in 4 Different Languages

1. German
Summ summ

2. Japanese
Boon boon

3. TURKISH
Vizzz

4. RUSSIAN
Zh-zh-zh

4
Biggest
and SMALLEST

1. Dogs
The smallest breed of dog is the chihuahua—the record-holder measures just 3.8 inches (9.65 cm) at the shoulder. A great Dane is the world's largest dog at 44 inches (111.8 cm) tall—over 11 times taller than the chihuahua.

2. Jellyfish
The smallest jellyfish is the highly venomous Irukandji jellyfish, which is only the size of a fingernail. The largest is the lion's mane jellyfish, 100 feet (30 m) long and 7.2 feet (2.2 m) across.

3. Primates
The smallest primate is Madame Berthe's mouse lemur, which is just 3.6 inches (9.2 cm) long and 1.1 ounces (30 g) in weight. The largest is the mighty eastern gorilla, 6 feet (1.85 m) tall and 465 pounds (210 kg).

4. Deer
The northern pudu is the world's smallest deer, just 14 inches (35 cm) tall and 13 pounds (6 kg). The biggest kind of deer is the moose, a whopping 1,765 pounds (800 kg) in weight and 8.5 feet (2.6 m) tall.

11 Animal Phobias
· · · · · · · · · · · ·

1. **Ailurophbia:** fear of cats
2. Arachnophobia: **fear of spiders**
3. **Bufonophobia:** fear of toads
4. Cynophobia: **fear of dogs**
5. **Equinophobia or hippophobia:** fear of horses
6. Herpetophobia: **fear of reptiles**
7. **Ichthyophobia:** fear of fish
8. Melissophobia or apiphobia: **fear of bees**
9. **Ophidiophobia:** fear of snakes
10. **Ranidaphobia:** fear of frogs
11. Zoophobia: **fear of animals**

4
FUNNY-LOOKING FISH

1. **Saw shark:** this shark's nose looks like a saw, edged with sharp saw teeth. It uses it to attack its prey.

2. **Barreleye fish:** barreleyes have transparent heads and tube-shaped eyes that stare upward, looking for prey.

3. **Winghead shark:** wingheads are a type of hammerhead shark, and have the widest heads of all—up to 3 feet (91 cm) wide.

4. **Swordfish:** this fish has a narrow bill as long and sharp as a sword, formed of the animal's upper jawbone.

12 KINDS OF SEAHORSE

There are over 50 different species of this oddly shaped marine fish, found mainly in shallow tropical and temperate salt water around the world. Here is a small selection.

1. **Spiny seahorse**
2. Big-bellied seahorse
3. **Narrow-bellied seahorse**
4. Giraffe seahorse
5. **Tiger-tail seahorse**
6. Long-snouted seahorse
7. **Short-snouted seahorse**
8. Bullneck seahorse
9. **Longnose seahorse**
10. Hedgehog seahorse
11. **Zebra seahorse**
12. Spotted seahorse

6 Animals with IMPRESSIVE HORNS

Horns, by the way, are different from antlers—they are extensions of the animal's skull, while antlers are made of dead bone that's shed and regrown every year.

1. **ALPINE IBEX**—huge, back-curving horns up to 4.5 feet (1.4 m) long.
2. **GIANT ELAND**—these impressive horns form a spiral, then taper to a sharp point.
3. **CAPE BUFFALO**—the horns meet in the middle to form a rock-hard shield across the animal's head.
4. **BLACKBUCK ANTELOPE**—the ringed, corkscrew-shaped horns can be nearly as tall as the antelope, up to 29.5 inches (75 cm).
5. **GIANT ELAND**—the biggest antelope in the world, with chunky, twisting horns.
6. **JACKSON'S CHAMELEON**—surprisingly, this chameleon has three horns, like a tiny, green Triceratops.

13 TYPES OF *Coral*

They might look like plants, but corals are tiny animals related to sea anemones and jellyfish. Hard corals have soft bodies and hard outer limestone skeletons, and live in colonies which act as a single organism. Over hundreds or thousands of years, coral colonies join together to form coral reefs. Here are a few kinds of these incredible creatures:

1. **Blue coral**
2. Brain coral
3. **Elkhorn coral**
4. Great star coral
5. **Grooved brain coral**
6. Lettuce coral
7. **Mountainous star coral**

8. Mustard hill coral
9. **Pillar coral**
10. Solitary disk coral
11. **Staghorn coral**
12. Table coral
13. **Tube coral**

7

CORAL REEF CREATURES

1. **Clown triggerfish:** spurts water at starfish to knock them off the coral, then eats them.

2. **Sea slug:** brightly colored to warn predators that it's not good to eat.

3. **Seahorse:** small fish with a horselike head.

4. **Hermit crab:** lives inside the abandoned shells of other animals.

5. **Giant clam:** can live for over a hundred years.

6. **Parrotfish:** eats coral —the hard parts are passed through the fish's body and come out as sand.

7. **Moray eel:** stays very still, then strikes suddenly at passing fish.

5 ANIMAL RAINFALLS

1. **Jellyfish rained on Bath, England, in 1894.**
2. Spiders rained on Goulburn, Australia, in 2015.
3. **Worms rained on Louisiana, USA, in 2007.**
4. Frogs rained on Odzaci, Serbia, in 2005 and on Rakoczifalva, Hungary, in 2010.
5. **Sardines regularly rain on Yoro, Honduras.**

5 SPECTACLED ANIMALS

All of these animals got their names because they have rings around their eyes, as though they're wearing glasses.

1. **Spectacled bear:** the only kind of bear that lives in South America.
2. **Spectacled owl:** the largest kind of tropical owl. It lives in Mexico and Central and South America.
3. **Spectacled caiman:** from the same family group as crocodiles, it has a spectacle-like ridge around its eyes. It lives in Central and South America.
4. **Spectacled cobra:** found in South Asia, it has a pattern on the back of its head that looks like a pair of glasses.
5. **Spectacled eider:** Arctic seaduck with white circles around its eyes.

3 Facts about ZEBRAS

1. There are three different kinds of zebra, which are closely related to horses and live in Africa: the plains zebra (the most common), Grevy's zebra (which is endangered), and the mountain zebra.

2. **No one is sure why zebras have stripes. No two zebras' stripes are the same, so the stripes might help them to recognize one another.**

3. Zebras can run at up to 40 mph (65 km/h). Speed helps them escape from predators including hyenas, cheetahs, and lions.

7

MIGRATORY *Birds*

About 40 percent of all the birds in the world migrate, flying seasonally to warmer places with more food available.

1. BLACK-HEADED BUNTING
Breeds in southeast Europe and parts of the Middle East, and migrates in winter to India and as far as southeast Asia.

2. WHITE STORK
Breeds in Europe and migrates to Africa for the winter.

3. CALLIOPE HUMMINGBIRD
Breeds in northwestern North America and spends the winter in Mexico.

4. RAINBOW BEE-EATER
Breeds in southern Australia and spends the winter farther north in Australasia.

5. NORTHERN SHOVELER
Breeds in North America, Europe, and northern Asia, and migrates to southern USA, South America, North Africa, and southern Asia in the winter.

6. SANDHILL CRANE
Breeds in Alaska, Canada, and Russia and flies south to southern USA and Mexico.

7. SNOW BUNTING
Breeds in the Arctic and spends the winter in central North America and Asia.

4

ANIMALS With *Built-in* Food Storage

1. Chipmunks stuff their cheeks with food to eat later.

2. Hamsters also have cheek pouches for storing food.

3. Honeypot ants store nectar, sap, and honeydew in a huge storage sac on the back of their bodies.

4. The black swallower is a deep-sea fish that can eat enormous meals and store them in its oversized stomach.

7 Very Loud ANIMALS

1. Blue whales, the biggest animals on Earth, make calls to one another that are louder than the sound of a jet engine. Because water carries sound farther than air, the calls can reach other whales hundreds of miles away.

2. Even louder, and in fact the loudest animal in the world, is the tiger pistol shrimp, which makes a sound louder than a gunshot.

3. Cicadas are the loudest insects. There are two kinds that are loudest of all—the greengrocer and yellow Monday cicadas.

4. The coqui frog from Puerto Rico makes a noise as loud as a pneumatic drill.

5. Howler monkeys' calls can be heard over 3 miles (5 km) away.

6. The kakapo, a flightless parrot from New Zealand, makes a booming call as loud as standing in front of a speaker at a rock concert.

7. Almost as loud, the male white bellbird from Brazil perches high in a tree and screeches to attract a mate.

7 Pet-themed *Museums*

1. **Cat Museum, Kuching, Malaysia**

2. Dog Collar Museum, Kent, UK

3. **The American Museum of the House Cat, North Carolina, USA**

4. Dachshund Museum, Passau, Germany

5. **Presidential Pet Museum, Annapolis, USA**

6. The American Kennel Club Museum of the Dog, New York City, USA

7. **Bunny Museum, Altadena, USA**

 ★ **10 KINDS OF WHALES**

1. **Beluga whale**
2. Blue whale
3. **Bowhead whale**
4. Fin whale
5. **Gray whale**

6. Humpback whale
7. **Minke whale**
8. Omura's whale
9. **Sei whale**
10. Sperm whale

8 Facts about ALPACAS

· · · · · · · · · · · · · · · · ·

1. Alpacas originate from the Andes in South America.

2. They are related to llamas and camels.

3. Alpacas are often kept for their soft wool.

4. It is thought they were originally bred as farm animals.

5. Adult alpacas weigh 100-200 pounds (45-90 kg).

6. There are two types of alpaca—huacaya alpaca and suri alpaca.

7. Alpacas eat mostly grass. They have no top front teeth!

8. Alpacas are herd animals and don't like to live alone.

3 Dimorphic Animals

Many animals are dimorphic—the males and females look different. In some species, the differences are extreme!

1. Southern elephant seal—males can weigh over 4.4 tons, eight times as much as females!

2. Blanket octopus—males are around 3/4 inch (2 cm) long, but females can grow up to 6 feet (1.8 m) and weigh up to 40,000 times more than males!

3. Lamprologus callipterus fish—the males are 12 times heavier than the females of this small fish species.

5 Tiny PYGMY ANIMALS

1. **Pygmy Japan pig seahorse:** up to $\frac{2}{3}$ inch (16 mm) long
2. **Brookesia micra chameleon:** up to 1.2 inches (30 mm) long
3. **Pygmy mouse lemur:** up to 2.6 inches (6.5 cm) long
4. **Pygmy marmoset:** up to 6.3 inches (16 cm) long
5. **Pygmy slow loris:** up to 10 inches (25 cm) long

3 Bigger PYGMY ANIMALS

1. **African pygmy goat:** up to 23 inches (58 cm) tall
2. **Pygmy marmoset:** up to 3 feet (91 cm) tall
3. **Borneo pygmy elephant:** up to 10 feet (3 m) tall

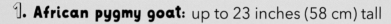
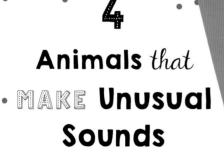

4 Animals that MAKE Unusual Sounds

1. The walnut sphinx caterpillar whistles like a bird when it feels threatened.

2. Male ostriches make a sound like an engine revving to attract females.

3. The grasshopper mouse makes a high-pitched howl, which has earned it the nickname "werewolf mouse"!

4. Lyrebirds mimic other birds' calls as well as man-made sounds such as car alarms, power tools, and camera clicks.

6 INCREDIBLE CHAMELEON FACTS

1. Chameleons are mostly found in Africa.

2. There are over 150 species of chameleon.

3. Chameleons can make their skin color lighter or darker to help them cool down or warm up.

4. They can show off bright colors to send messages to other chameleons.

5. Chameleons can move their eyes in two directions at once, meaning they get a 360-degree view to alert them to danger.

6. Chameleons have incredibly long, sticky tongues which they flick out of their mouth to catch insects.

8 FACTS About RHINOS

1. Rhinoceroses (rhinos) are found in Southern Africa.

2. Rhinos are herbivores—they don't eat meat.

3. The two most common types of rhino are black rhinos and white rhinos.

4. A white rhino can weigh up to 4.4 tons.

5. Rhinos have two horns on their face, one bigger than the other.

6. Black rhinos are in danger of becoming extinct due to hunters who take their horns.

7. Rhino horns can grow up to 3 inches (7.5 cm) a year.

8. Rhinos use their horns to fight or protect their young.

6 Animals that BREATHE Through THEIR SKIN

1. Earthworms **2. Salamanders**
3. Frogs **4. Toads** **5.** Newts
6. Sea snakes

6 ANIMALS that Eat their own POOP

If you want to be scientific about it, coprophagia is the special term for poop eating.

1. A mother dog licks her puppies to make them poop and pee, then eats it. Puppies sometimes eat poop, possibly because there's something in it that's missing in their diet.

2. Chimpanzees occasionally eat their poop, most likely because some of the food has only been partly digested.

3. Rabbits and hares produce a special type of soft, dark, tarry poop (in contrast to their normal poop, which is brown and hard). They eat the special poop and digest all of the nutrients they missed the first time around.

4. Baby elephants don't eat their own poop, but they do eat the dung of their mothers and other elephants. It helps the babies establish healthy bacteria in their guts.

5. Mountain beavers aren't beavers and they don't live in mountains— but they do eat their own poop.

6. Cassowaries are large flightless birds from southeast Asia and Australia. They eat their poop because it usually contains half-digested fruit, which still has plenty of nutritional value.

8 Cannibal Animals

As well as the animals that eat their mates, all of these animals have been known to eat their own kind.

1. Both male and female chimpanzees have been spotted eating their babies or attacking other chimp communities and killing and eating them.

2. Rabbit mothers will eat their babies if danger threatens.

3. Polar bears have been seen killing and eating young polar bears in the wild.

4. The female crab spider gives her offspring a good start in life—she is eaten by her newly hatched babies.

5. Male and female hamsters sometimes eat weaker young.

6. If a mother scorpion can't find enough bugs or grubs to eat, she sometimes eats a few of her own babies.

7. Sand tiger sharks are cannibals before they're born—the bigger embryos eat the smaller ones while they are still inside their mother.

8. Ground crickets from Zimbabwe eat the dead bodies of other ground crickets.

10 Kinds of CONSTRICTING SNAKE

These snakes kill prey by coiling around a victim and squeezing tighter and tighter until it can't breathe. Some can reach an enormous size—the biggest are the green anaconda from South America and the reticulated python, which can grow to 30 feet (9 m). There are lots of different kinds, including these:

1. **Ball python**
2. Blood python
3. **Boa constrictor**
4. Carpet python
5. **Emerald tree boa**
6. Green anaconda
7. **Rainbow boa**
8. Reticulated python
9. **Rubber boa**
10. Sand boa

7 BALD MAMMALS

1. **Red uakari—Amazon monkey with long reddish or white fur and a bright-red bald head.**

2. Peruvian Inca orchid —Peru's national dog, which can be hairy or hairless. The hairless kind has wispy fur on its head and tail.

3. **Skinny pig —hairless guinea pigs.**

4. Vultures—many different kinds of vulture have a bald head.

5. **Naked mole rat—this burrowing African rodent is pink and hairless.**

6. Sphynx cat—this domestic cat was bred to be bald.

7. **Hippopotamus—hippos would only be weighed down in water if they were hairy, so, like marine mammals, they've evolved to be bald.**

5 FACTS about HUMANS

1. **Humans and chimpanzees shared a common ancestor about 6 million years ago. The two species share nearly 99 percent of their DNA.**

2. Human beings are social animals. The average person is capable of recognizing 5,000 unique faces.

3. **We live all over the world—although no one lives in Antarctica permanently.**

4. About 74,000 years ago, modern humans nearly became extinct as a result of extreme climate change. Now there are over 7 billion humans living on the planet.

5. **Humans left Earth's atmosphere for the first time in 1961 when Russian cosmonaut Yuri Gagarin went into orbit around the planet. Since then, people have traveled to the Moon, and the next destination is the planet Mars.**

INDEX

Page numbers in **bold** indicate a complete list.